BASIC ✳ ESSENTIALS™
CAMPING

Dedication

To my friend, Bob Brown, who continues to camp out but avowedly hates every minute of it!

Acknowledgments

A special thanks to Dr. Bill Forgey, who at the start, believed in the idea of this book. To my previous editor, Tom Todd, who has always been willing to make last minute changes.

Help Us Keep This Guide Up to Date

Every effort has been made by the author and editors to make this guide as accurate and useful as possible. However, many things can change after a guide is published—new products and information become available, regulations change, techniques evolve, etc.

We would love to hear from you concerning your experience with this guide and how you feel it could be improved and be kept up to date. While we may not be able to respond to all comments and suggestions, we'll take them to heart and we'll also make certain to share them with the author. Please send your comments and suggestions to the following address:

The Globe Pequot Press
Reader Response/Editorial Department
P.O. Box 833
Old Saybrook, CT 06475

Or you may e-mail us at:

editorial@globe-pequot.com

Thanks for your input, and happy travels!

BASIC ESSENTIALS™ SERIES

BASIC ✳ ESSENTIALS™

CAMPING

SECOND EDITION

CLIFF JACOBSON

The Globe Pequot Press

Old Saybrook, Connecticut

Illustrations by Cliff Moen
Cover design by Lana Mullen
Cover photo: Tom Todd
Text & Layout design by Casey Shain

Photo credits: Page 3, Cascade Designs (bottom) and Slumberjack (top); page 7, Kelty (top, bottom) and Eureka (middle); page 9, Lowe Alpine Systems (left, middle) and Pearl Izumi (right); page 11, Five Ten (top), Montrail (middle) and Salomon (bottom); page 13, Kelty (far left, far right) and Lowe Alpine systems (middle left, middle right); page 17, Idaho Knife Works (top; photo by M. Santostefano) and Grohmann Knives (bottom); page 20, Trail Blazer; page 21, Dawn Marketing/ Sawvivor (bottom) and Fast Bucksaw (top); page 28, Mountain Safety Research; page 36, Nalgene; page 67, Garmin Corporation.

Library of Congress Cataloging-in-Publication Data

Jacobson, Cliff.
    Basic essentials: camping / by Cliff Jacobson.—2nd ed.
        p. cm. —(Basic essentials series)
    Includes index.
    ISBN 0-7627-0427-6
      1. Camping.   2. Camping—Equipment and supplies.   I. Title
GV191.7.J326 1999
796.54—dc21   98-54365
                                              CIP

♻ Printed on recycled paper
Manufactured in Quebec, Canada
Second Edition/First Printing

Introduction

I discovered the joys of camping at the age of twelve in a rustic Scout camp set deep in the Michigan woods. It was 1952, just before the dawn of nylon tents and 60/40 parkas. Aluminum canoes were hot off the Grumman forms, though I'd never seen one. Deep down, I believed they'd never replace the glorious Old Towns and Thompsons.

Like most kids my age, I had little money for outdoor gear. What I earned by picking pop bottles off the roadway went for a secondhand bike or a Randolph Scott movie. My camping outfit was carefully assembled from a ragtag assortment of military surplus and Salvation Army store items. I knew only one kid who had equipment that was new. Once I saved enough to buy an official Boy Scout knife, which in those days came with good carbon steel blades and a metal BSA insignia.

One Christmas Dad gave me an all-steel Scout handaxe, which came complete with tooled leather sheath and varnished wood scales. For twenty years thereafter I proudly carried it on all my hiking and canoe trips. It was my edge for making fires on a rainy day. Early on, I decided that those who badmouthed hatchets simply lacked the skills to use them right. I still retain that conviction, as you'll see in Chapter 2.

On my fourteenth birthday I received another treasured gift—a solid brass M 71 Primus stove, which, at five dollars was a genuinely expensive gift.

These items, along with an army surplus wool sleeping bag and poncho, comprised my store of camping items. Everything fit nicely into a tan canvas packsack and together tipped the scale at barely 20 pounds. To this, add a week's worth of dehydrated Seidel trail foods, a handful of big stick matches and a spartan change of clothes, and I was ready for the great adventure.

At last I owned all the tripping gear I'd ever need. What boy could be more fortunate? Admittedly, I yearned for an army down-and-feathers sleeping bag—the wool one I had was adequate only in the heat of summer. But no matter: With an extra blanket and knitted sweater, I got by. Even in snow. After all, being a little cold was part of the camping game, wasn't it?

My bible on how to camp was the *Boy Scout Handbook*, which, I was told, contained absolutely everything one could want to know about the great outdoors. It was all there—from how to trench a tent and build a bed of pine boughs to the construction of rope-lashed furniture and emergency dwellings. Axmanship was serious stuff, so it was treated as a separate chapter.

Environmental concerns? There were none. Not that we didn't care, you understand. We just didn't see anything wrong with cutting trees and restructuring the soil to suit our needs. Given the equipment of the day, reshaping the land was the most logical way to make outdoor life bearable.

Litter, of course, was another matter. We proudly packed out *everything* we (and anyone else) brought in. We were Boy Scouts, not slobs!

In 1958, Calvin Rutstrum brought out his first book, *The Way of the Wilderness*. Suddenly, there was new philosophy afield. Calvin knew the days of trenched tents and bough beds were numbered. His writings challenged readers to think before they cut, to use an air mattress instead of a spruce bed. Wilderness camping was in proud transition. New products—nylon, Dacron, stainless steel, and vinyl—were already fragmenting the monopolies enjoyed by cotton, wool, and canvas. Outfitters by the thousands sold (or burned) their cotton tents and joined the nylon revolution.

Suddenly the emphasis had shifted from *skills* to *things*. Knowing how was no longer good enough. Everyone needed a plethora of new gear—down sleeping bags and foam sleeping pads; Swiss Army knives with a tool for everything; waterproof boots with Vibram lugs; two-piece rain suits with clever hoods that moved with the turn of a head; polypropylene socks and underwear and pile pullovers; erector-set tents that needed no staking; Gore-Tex suits that breathed in the rain; color-matched designer clothes that looked good at the All-Stars game; and tiny trail stoves that ran on canister of liquid butane.

Suddenly I felt quite inadequate, like a peasant in Camelot.

Calvin Rutstrum summed it up one foggy morning on a mid-September day. I'd driven up to meet him at his wilderness cabin on the North shore of Lake Superior. Cal had built the place himself, every inch of it. No need to pour a concrete slab; a mirror-flat shelf of slate was good enough. The double cabin was artfully constructed from native pine. And it was solid!

As Cal poured coffee, I baited him by pulling from its stuff sack a polyester-filled sleeping bag I'd purchased for my wife.

"Whatcha think of these new poly bags?" I asked. "They dry really fast—could be a lifesaver if you get your down bag wet."

With that, Rutstrum, in his early eighties, slammed down his cup on the wood-pinned table and splashed brown liquid onto the varnished wood. Slowly he rose, his set jaw and steel gray eyes poised in anger.

"Damn!" he called loudly: "I've canoed and camped for nigh on seventy years and I've never gotten my down bag wet. Never. Not ever! Those who get stuff wet on a trip need help. They need to learn how to camp!"

I could have cheered!

It seems as though high-tech gear and high-powered salesmanship have become a substitute for rock solid camping skills. Chemical fire-starters take the place of correct fire making; indestructible canoes are the solution to hitting rocks; blizzard-proof tents become the answer to one's inability to stormproof conventional designs. And the what-if-you-get-your-down-bag-wet syndrome attracts new converts each year. In the end only the manufacturers win. For even the best gear falls short of expectations without proper know-how.

And that, friends, is what this book is all about. No pressure to buy the new, discard the old. Just a mash of proven procedures to enhance your camping trips.

What's New About This New Edition?

Lots of stuff! Even if you've read the first edition of this book, you'll still find lots of new material to keep the pages turning. There are luscious new recipes and slick tricks for managing meals on miserable days, new ways to storm-proof the popular self-supporting dome tents, and tips for rigging tarps in big winds. You'll discover that the recommended procedures you should follow when confronted by a bear—and when protecting your food from one—have changed considerably. You'll want to read this section carefully before your next campout.

There's new ammunition to help you win your battle with bugs and bad weather as well as tips for sleeping soundly on rough ground. Check out the all-new chapter on the dangers of camping out.

If you like what you read and want to learn even more about the topics covered in this book, look for the new editions of my other books: *Camping's Top Secrets, Basic Essentials™ Cooking in the Outdoors, Basic Essentials™ Map and Compass,* and *Basic Essentials™ Knots for the Outdoors.*

I'm proud of this new revision. It's chock-full of all the important things you really need to know to enjoy camping out.

How to Use Your Gear Effectively

I recently checked the contents of a popular backpacking book and found that around 90 percent of its pages were devoted to the selection of equipment. There were full chapters on Choosing the Sleeping Bag, A Tent for All Seasons, and Getting Booted Up. Except for some obvious advice about pitching camp on high ground and packing clothes in waterproof bags, there was precious little of value to crow about. Right then, I vowed to take a more practical tack in this book.

Certainly, proper equipment is important to a quality outdoor experience. Only a fool would suggest otherwise. But the engineering specifics of every product are available free from the manufacturer, and detailed equipment evaluations are the annual rule in most every outdoor magazine. And if you're still confused over what variables go into selecting a great tent or sleeping bag, just ask the folks who sell outdoor gear at first-rate camping shops. Most of these young men and women are quite knowledgeable, and just about all are active hikers, bikers, canoeists, and skiers. High-tech camping equipment is not usually sold on commission, which means the purveyors will react honestly to your concerns.

So rather than clutter this chapter with equipment trivia that is readily available elsewhere, I'll suggest some ways to make your good gear perform at its best.

Sleeping Bags

Selecting Your Sleeping Bag

What you choose depends on how classy you want to travel and how much you want to spend. At the top of the list are three-hundred

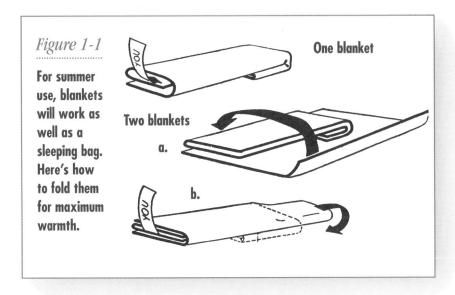

Figure 1-1

For summer use, blankets will work as well as a sleeping bag. Here's how to fold them for maximum warmth.

One blanket

Two blankets

a.

b.

dollar down bags, while at the bottom are twenty-nine dollar astro-fill specials that are no better than paired blankets. And speaking of blankets: A set of airy acrylic or loose-woven wool blankets, sandwiched à la Boy Scout style (Figure 1-1), makes a perfectly good bed for typical summer campouts. If cost *is* an object, here's the place to cut: There's no sense buying three-section protection if you'll use it only in the blistering heat of summer. Most campers own bags that are too warm. Only if you're heading to the far north should you consider the merits of an autumn-rated (25 degree Fahrenheit) sleeping bag.

For car camping (which really can't be called sleeping out), any sleeping bag will do. Otherwise, my vote goes to a roomy mummy bag with a fully formed head and boxed (raised) foot (Figure 1-2). Be sure the bag has a two-way zipper that runs from foot to chin.

In sleeping bags, more than any other camping product, you get exactly what you pay for. At this writing, one hundred dollars will put you into a quality synthetic bag. Twice this will buy a good down bag.

So which one is for you? First, be aware that *good* down will outlast the best Polarguard/Hollofil/Quallofil by decades. Conscientious bag makers suggest a useful life of around five years for a heavily used synthetic bag. With down bags, the nylon shell goes first. How long? Well, one of my down bags is now thirty years old, and it's still going strong!

As to the argument that down bags are hard to dry when they get wet on a camping trip, rethink the logic of Calvin Rutstrum. If you pack your bag as I suggest, you'll never get it wet. Not ever!

The recommended procedure for waterproofing the sleeping bag is to stuff it into a nylon sack that has first been lined with a plastic bag. This is foolish advice! Every time you stuff the bag into the plastic sack, you stretch and abrade the plastic. In no time, tears—and leaks—develop. Some experts know this and so suggest that you carry some extra plastic bags, which is even more absurd.

Here's a better way: First, stuff the bag into its nylon sack (which need not be watertight), then set the sack inside a sturdy plastic bag. Pleat and twist the end of the plastic bag, fold it over and secure it with a loop of shock-cord. Then, place this unit into an oversize nylon sack (again, which need not be waterproof). Note that the delicate plastic liner—which is the only real water barrier—is protected from abrasion on both sides!

It's especially important to adopt this procedure if you'll be tying your sleeping bag onto the outside of a pack frame, where it will be constantly exposed to the weather. You'll also appreciate the extra abrasion resistance of the sandwiched construction when you hike through thorns or brambles. On one occasion I sliced through an outer stuff sack while hiking in rough country.

Figure 1-2

A mummy sleeping bag (top) and a square-cut sleeping bag (bottom).

In camp. Some authorities advise you to lay out your sleeping bag and fluff it to full loft well in advance of bedtime. This is supposed to increase its insulative value. Hogwash! Better to leave the bag stuffed and protected until you need it. A good sleeping bag will fluff to full loft within sixty seconds after it's pulled from the sack. Just give it a good shake before you climb in.

Washing Your Sleeping Bag

First, never dry-clean your sleeping bag—down or synthetic. Handwashing is the recommended procedure, though machine washing—in a front loader only—works just as well.

As to soaps, any liquid detergent will do. Powdered detergents are okay if you can get them to dissolve thoroughly.

HERE ARE THE RULES:

1. Use warm or cold water only. Excess heat will destroy any sleeping bag.

2. Use half as much liquid detergent as you think you need.

3. Remove the spun-dry bag from the washer and place it in an extractor (a high speed centrifuge, available at laundromats). One pass through the extractor will remove nearly all the water.

4. Dry the bag at a low heat setting in a large commercial dryer. Be sure the dryer actually puts out low heat. If it doesn't, jam a magazine over the safety button so you can run the door ajar. Note: A terry cloth towel placed in the dryer with the sleeping bag will speed drying.

That's all there is to it! I wash my sleeping bags once a year.

Trail Mattresses

A mattress will smooth the way for old bones and warm your backside when you sleep on cold ground. There are four basic types of trail mattresses.

Air mattress. Except for car camping, the traditional air mattress is extinct. Except in the heat of summer, air mattresses cannot be used with down sleeping bags. Body weight compresses an air mattress down to near-zero thickness (synthetics are less affected): If the ground is cold, your backside is, too! If you want to be comfortable and warm, place a thin, closed-cell foam pad on top of your air mattress.

Closed-cell foam. Closed-cell foam insulates efficiently and is waterproof, inexpensive, and unaffected by punctures . . . and not very comfortable. It's the foam of choice for subzero camping, however, where a mattress failure could be serious. Three-eighths of an inch is thick enough for summer: double that for use on snow. It is the best pad for children, especially those who may wet their beds.

Fabric-covered open-cell foam. A trail mattress of this type is basically a huge sponge covered with nylon or cotton. This design is reasonably comfortable, inexpensive, unaffected by punctures, and not waterproof. Open-cell foam is bulky when rolled, and it doesn't insulate as well as closed-cell foam.

Air-filled foam pads. The Therma-Rest began the revolution, now there's lots of competition. Basically, these units consist of a low-density (soft and cushy) open-cell foam that's sealed in an envelope of vinyl and nylon. An oversized plastic valve controls the air flow. Open the valve and the pad inflates itself. Close the valve to lock in the air. The result is a very comfortable, incredibly warm (suitable for subzero use), and surprisingly reliable mattress.

Some Trail Mattress Tips

Make a tough cotton or light wool cover for your air-filled foam pad. The cover will protect the pad from punctures and keep it from sliding on the slippery nylon tent floor. In hot weather the cotton or wool material will be more comfortable to sleep on than the non-porous nylon shell of the air pad.

Don't use a cotton cover in winter: Damp cotton will draw heat from your body. Winter covers should be made from pure polyester or tightly woven wool.

A crinkly "space blanket" (every discount store has them), set silver side up under your foam pad will add considerable warmth to your sleeping system.

If you find yourself sleeping on an uncomfortable incline, level out your sleeping system by placing folded clothes beneath your air mat or foam pad. This method can make an otherwise intolerable sleeping situation quite bearable.

Tip. **If you are stuck with an inclined site, pitch your tent perpendicular to the drop (one side lower than the other), rather than parallel to it with the entrance high, as suggested in most camping books. It's easier to level a "sunken side" than a "lowered end." Figure 1-3 shows why.**

Tents

You don't need a sophisticated high-altitude tent for general camping. Any simple forest tent will do if it has a bathtub floor (no perimeter seams at ground level) and a waterproof fly that stakes nearly to the ground. The fly must cover every seam and floor corner. If you rely on glue (seam sealant) to waterproof exposed seams, you're just asking for trouble. A vestibule (alcove) is important: It provides a place to store equipment out of the weather. Vestibules also seal the entryway of a tent from blowing rain and snow.

Each person needs about 2½ by 7 feet just to stretch out. Add an additional half foot (3 feet x 7½ feet) plus headroom enough to dress, and you enter the realm of comfort. A tent used for general camping should be relatively commodious—a 6-foot by 8-foot floor plan (commonly referred to as a 3–4 person tent) is ideal for two. Weight? Under twelve pounds, and the lighter the better. Serious backpackers will opt for the lightest, most compact tent they can get, which may or may not be a good idea. If you have to spend the day weatherbound in a doghousy little shelter with no room to sit upright, you'll wish you'd brought a bigger tent. Your tent is your home away from home, so this is not the place to cut corners.

You'll pay much more for high-tech geometrics (domes, tunnels, and such) than for simple-to-sew but reliable A-frames. If you're going

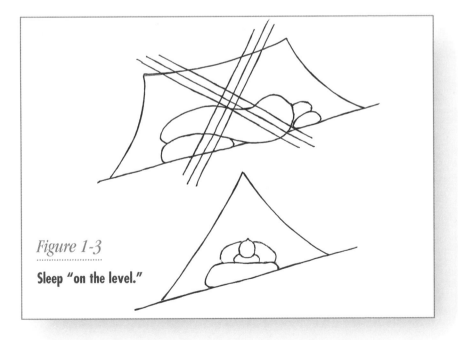

Figure 1-3

Sleep "on the level."

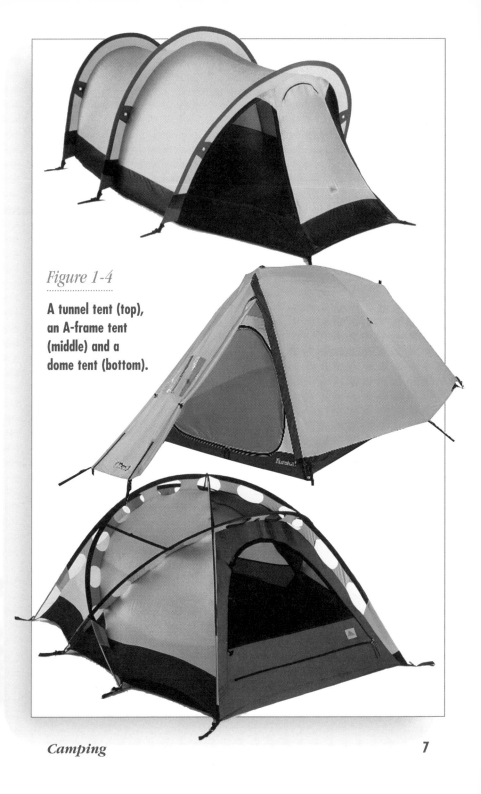

Figure 1-4

A tunnel tent (top),
an A-frame tent
(middle) and a
dome tent (bottom).

to the mountains and need the reliability of a windproof tent, by all means get one. But if your camping will be confined to the tree line, choose a more moderate design—one that enables you to keep your sanity in an all-day rain. See Figure 1-4 for some examples of types of tents.

Don't leave home without installing a plastic groundcloth *inside* your tent. The groundsheet will prevent pooled surface water, which wicks through floor seams (and in time, worn floor fabric), from entering your sleeping area. Don't place the plastic sheet under the tent as advised by some tentmakers—rain water may become trapped between it and the floor and be pressure-wicked (from body weight) through the nylon fabric into the tent. You'll really have a sponge party if this happens! Use of an interior groundcloth is the best wet-weather tip I can give you. On numerous occasions, this feature has saved me from an unexpected midnight bath.

Almost any tent can be made to survive a severe storm, if you know how to rig it. Chapter 6 shows you how.

Tent Poles and Stakes

Tent poles should be made of *aluminum*, never of fiberglass or plastic, which can break. *Wands* (not supporting members), which are used to hold out awnings and vents, are an exception. All poles should be shock-corded for easy assembly.

SOME TENT POLE TIPS:

Tent poles won't jam together and will slide more easily through pole sleeves if you polish the joints (a one-time effort) with 400-grit wet sandpaper and then wipe them with a cloth sprayed with liquid silicone.

To release pole sections that are stuck together, heat the joint lightly in the flame of your trail stove. The joint will expand and the poles will part easily.

Tent stakes: Twelve inch-long arrow-shaft aluminum stakes or "staples" (u-shaped stakes) hold best in sand; sharp aluminum skewers are good for compacted soil; and narrow steel wire stakes are ideal for rocky ground. Carry a variety of tent stakes so you'll always have what works best.

Tip. **8-inch long aluminum concrete nails make acceptable low-cost tent stakes. The heavy steel-and-plastic "U-pound 'em" stakes sold at discount stores are useful only on big, semi-permanent canvas tents.**

Special stakes are unnecessary for camping on snow or sand. Conventional aluminum stakes can be buried, or guylines wound about wooden sticks, then buried. Tin can lids (with the edges peened in for safety) make good snow stakes. Run the guylines through holes in the center and bury the lids.

Clothing and Rain Gear

You don't need outdoor designer wear to enjoy camping. Simply avoid wearing cotton, except in the height of summer heat, and you'll do fine. Blue jeans are a particularly bad choice: Once they get wet and cold, they stay that way. A number of deaths due to hypothermia (see Chapter 8) have been traced to the wearing of this article.

A lot of very experienced campers do all their shopping at army surplus and discount stores, where they find good-quality items at low prices. Military woolens, inexpensive acrylics, and polyester pile are the favored regimen, as are cotton/polyester fatigues and chinos.

Figure 1-5

Rain jackets and a pair of rain pants.

A breathable nylon jacket is essential to stern the biting winds, and don't forget polypropylene, polyester, or wool long johns when the need arises. Be aware that polypropylene absorbs body odors and smells awful after a few days on the trail. Polyesters are much better. My wife, Sue Harings, is more conscious of odors that I am, and she insists that I recommend Thermax® and its relative Thermostat™ by name. Sue says that most of her friends also prefer these "sweet-smelling" fabrics. Cabela's Inc. (see Appendix) has a large selection of men's, women's, and unisex styles.

Don't thumb your nose at traditional wool garments. Unlike synthetics, tightly woven wool resists sparks and wind and will repel a substantial rain, and it's not dissolved by harsh chemicals (such as insect repellents). Wool also keeps you warm when it's soaked with water (synthetics may need to be wrung out). Despite all the hoopla about synthetics, pure virgin wool remains the strongest, most reliable fiber you can wear in mean weather. Super soft, non-scratching woolens (merino) are available. Filson and Pendleton make the very best wool garments.

A change of clothes from nose to toes is the rule, whether you're going for a weekend or a month. Everything should fit easily into an 8-inch by 12-inch nylon stuff sack.

Rain gear (Figure 1-5) should be uncomplicated. A two-piece rain suit is better than a poncho, which dribbles through, or a knee-length shirt (cagoule), which is awkward for everything except lazing about camp. The best buys on rainwear are usually found in industrial supply stores where construction workers shop. The new construction-grade rain suits are strong, light, and wondrously inexpensive. They'll keep you plenty dry, even though they lack the exquisite tailoring, multiple pockets, and exotic hoods (which you really don't need) of high-tech camp store garments.

Gore-Tex garments are "waterproof and breathable," if you specify the Rainwear Without Compromise label. Gore-Tex outfits are very expensive, however, and they require more care than coated fabrics. Gore-Tex shines best in transitional (snow/sleet/rain) weather.

Do not wear your rain gear for wind protection, as is commonly advised. Any item that is frequently worn will eventually develop holes. Wear your nylon shell jacket for wind and keep the polycoated stuff for its intended purpose. Always store rain clothes in a nylon sack to eliminate the abrasion that results from stuffing these garments into packsacks.

What you wear under rain gear is important. A light polypropylene or wool shirt will eliminate the clammy feeling that results from wearing waterproof clothing next to the skin.

So you're taking the children. No sense spending a bundle on clothing that will be outgrown in a season. *Acrylics* is the key word here. They are very inexpensive and dry almost instantly after a rain. A light, non-allergenic acrylic sweater worn next to the skin makes a fine underwear top for chilly weather. Again, avoid blue jeans: Cotton/polyester slacks dry faster and are cheaper. Rain gear is easy: A cut-down plastic poncho worn over a waterproof nylon jacket (double protection plus dry sleeves) will keep a youngster dry in the worst storms. Add a plastic souwester hat and rubber boots, and your little one is set for a delightful day afield.

Footwear

See Figure 1-6. The trend is to very lightweight boots for all but the most demanding applications. No knowledgeable hiker I know would be caught dead wearing the five-pound Vibram lug monstrosities that were so popular two decades ago. Now footwear rules are simple: wear the lightest, most flexible boot you can find. Exceptions are mountaineering and winter travel. If you need a really waterproof shoe, go for all-rubber or shoe-pack (leather top/rubber bottom) construction.

Here's an easy way to break in leather boots: Fill each boot with lukewarm tap water and allow the water to sit in the boot no more than fifteen seconds. Pour out the water, then walk the boots dry.

Figure 1-6

Lightweight boot

Middleweight boot

Heavyweight boot

Afterwards rub in a generous amount of leather preservative. Clean your boots regularly with saddle soap and re-apply preservative as needed.

Wear two pairs of socks in your boots. The outer pair should be made from heavy wool (at least 75 percent); the inner pair of lightweight wool or polypropylene (these are marvelous!). Wear the light liners *inside out* so that seams are away from your foot. This one precaution will eliminate most blisters. Liners should be changed daily. Outer socks may be worn two or three days, depending on your level of activity.

Packs

What you need depends entirely on your tripping style. For backpacking on relatively good trails, the aluminum-frame outfit reigns supreme. Rock scrambling requires more dexterity; hence, the development of the "soft pack" with internal stays. And for canoeing, nothing beats the venerable Duluth pack (Figure 1-7), which is nothing more than a canvas envelope with three closing straps. There are also a number of specialized packsacks designed for technical rock climbing and day meandering. The salespeople at any good equipment store will overwhelm you with the specifics of design and fit.

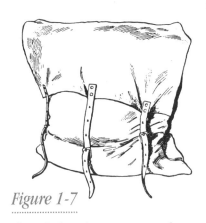

Figure 1-7

The Duluth pack, a canvas envelope that measures 24 by 30 inches, is the preferred pack for canoeing.

How to pack your pack. Now that most packs come with internal or external frames (see Figure 1-8), the science of proper packing has all but vanished. And that's too bad, because there is an efficient way to do things.

Proper packing begins with effective waterproofing. Now write this in technicolor: *Regardless of the manufacturer's claims, my pack is not waterproof!* Even double-coated pack fabrics are not foolproof. After all, there are seams. And fabrics do wear. The slightest scratch will allow a leak.

So start by lining your pack with a large plastic bag. Inside this, place a light fabric abrasion liner of some sort. The liner need not be waterproof—sheer polypropylene or nylon taffeta will do. Its only purpose is to absorb the abrasion that results from stuffing gear deep

BASIC ESSENTIALS

Figure 1-8
....

An external-frame pack
(far-left), two internal-
frame packs (middle),
and a frameless
daypack (right).

into the pack. The sandwich principle is the same as that recommended for packing the sleeping bag.

Exterior pack pockets must also be waterproofed. Zip-lock bags
are one solution; the pack rain coat—a tailored poly-coated nylon
apron which fits over the pack—is another. In camp, a giant plastic
garbage bag will protect everything from the worst rain.

Principles of packing. For general hiking, you want the weight
as close to your back and as high as possible. This means the sleeping
bag and foam pad go on the bottom, followed by clothing and sun-
dries. Reserve the top shelf for food, tent, and cooking gear.

Rock scrambling demands a lower load, though one which still
hugs your body. Frameless packs (Figure 1-8) are best loaded flat
(horizontally) to assure that soft items are evenly distributed along
the back and not massed together where they'll do no good.

Camping   **13**

Packing the tent. Here's your most obstinate load: Invariably the poles will be too long to fit in the pack. Most hikers respond by simply setting the lengthy tent bag under the closing flap of their packsack, which is hardly a good idea for these reasons: 1) It raises the load too high, which may unbalance the hiker; 2) the tent is exposed to the elements and thorny vegetation; 3) rain can get into the pack by working its way under the badly sealed closing flap.

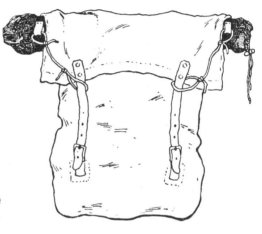

Figure 1-9

Pack the tent and poles separately. Set the pole and stake bag just under the pack flap and run the closing straps of the pack flap through loops of nylon cord sewn to the ends of the pole bag.

FAR BETTER TO PACK TENT AND POLES SEPARATELY AS FOLLOWS *(see Figure 1-9)*:

1. Stuff (my preference) or roll the tent, without stakes and poles, and place it in an oversize nylon bag. Pack poles and stakes in a separate nylon bag with drawstring closure.

2. Pack the tent between the waterproof plastic pack liner and the tightly rolled fabric abrasion liner. This will isolate it from the dry gear below. Set the pole and stake bag just under the pack flap and run the closing straps of the pack flap through loops of nylon cord sewn to the ends of the pole bag (or simply tie these cords to the pack frame).

3. Cinch the pack flap down tightly. The nylon cords keep the pole bag from sliding out beneath the pack flap.

Rain Fly (Tarp)

A 10-foot by 10-foot nylon rain tarp, tightly pitched between two trees, will enable you to prepare meals, make repairs, and otherwise enjoy a rainy day. The rain tarp is one of the most essential and over-looked items on a camping trip. Chapter 6 provides an in-depth look at how to rig it.

Stove

A stove is essential in all but the most infrequented areas. I prefer the self-contained single burner gasoline models, though the small two-burner Colemans are your best buy. The stove is so important, I've allotted a full chapter to it.

Toys

A butane lighter, flashlight, Sierra cup for a ladle, pot lifter or pliers, duct tape, rope and parachute cord, and a miniature sewing kit will suffice for the short trip. Extended stays require a full battery of sup-portive toys—everything from instant epoxy to leather replacement gaskets for the stove.

It's impossible to describe all you need to have—and need to know—in a chapter of this length. So don't neglect your studies. Read every book on camping you can find before you take to the back-country, and keep abreast of new developments by attending outdoor seminars. After all, it's one thing to own good gear; it's another to know how to use it effectively.

The Cutting Edge

I n the 1920s there were the sheath knife and full-size axe. By 1950 the common jackknife and three-quarter-length axe were in style. The 1970s brought forth the red-handled Swiss Army knife. In the 1980s lock-back knives were popular; now the trend is to serrated tactical knives (which are generally useless for camping) and multipurpose tools like the Leatherman and Gerber multipliers, and no axe at all.

Somewhere in their vacillation, campers have overlooked an important fact: Slicing cheese, splitting kindling, and other knife-related chores are about the same today as a century ago. It follows then that your choice of edged tools should—with appropriate modifications—reflect these similarities.

HERE'S MY FORMULA FOR A CAMP KNIFE:

1. Enough length (4- to 5-inch blade) to slice meat and cheese and reach deep into the peanut butter jar without getting gunked up.

2. A thin, flat-ground blade for effortless slicing.

Nearly all knives sold for outdoor use have blades that are too thick. One-eighth inch across the spine is the *maximum* thickness permissible for a utility knife, no matter how delicate the edge. Try slicing a tomato with the typical hunting knife and you'll see why.

The primary camp knife may be a fixed blade or folding model. You'll pay more for a good folder than for a sheath knife of similar length.

If your taste runs to folding knives, select a model with a 3- to 4-inch long, thin, flat-ground blade. If you want a razor-sharp edge that's easy to maintain, choose carbon steel over stainless. The best stainless blades are very good, but they can't compare to good tool steel knives for ease-of-sharpening and holding an edge.

Figure 2-1

The Cliff Knife (above) and Grohmann's Large Camper Knife (left).

Invariably, you'll need two knives for camping—a thin-ground kitchen style model for preparing foods and a substantial multi-purpose folder of some sort. In case you're wondering, my favorite camp knife is the "Cliff Knife," which I designed when I couldn't find a suitable replacement for my worn-out tool steel Gerber shorty (see Figure 2-1). My Cliff Knife has a wafer-thin, 4.3-inch blade of L6 tool steel, and it's custom made by Idaho Knife Works (see Appendix). I also like the Grohmann #2 "Trout and Bird" knife (4-inch blade) in carbon steel (don't get stainless). The carbon steel model is available from the Duluth Pack store in Duluth, Minnesota (see Appendix).

Sharpening. (See Figure 2-2.) Never use an electrical sharpener or one of those mechanical wheeled gadgets sold at supermarkets. You'll ruin the knife beyond repair! Instead, get a synthetic diamond

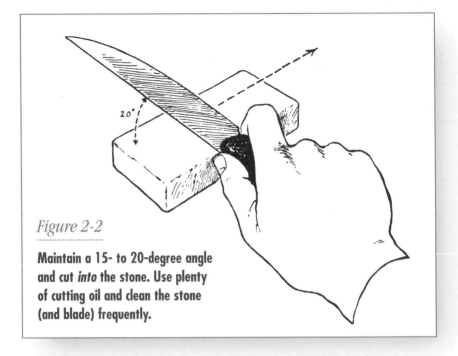

Figure 2-2
....

Maintain a 15- to 20-degree angle and cut *into* the stone. Use plenty of cutting oil and clean the stone (and blade) frequently.

stone (first choice) and/or a medium-grit *soft* Arkansas stone. If you want the finest razor edge, obtain a *hard* Arkansas stone as well.

Maintain a light film of cutting oil on the natural stones (use water on diamond stones) to float away steel particles. Raise the back of the blade 15 to 20 degrees and cut into the stone, as illustrated.

Clean the stone and blade frequently and apply new oil during the sharpening process. I generally take four strokes per side and apply new oil (first, cleaning off the old) every thirty strokes or so. When sharpening is complete, I strop the blade on leather to produce a razor-fine edge.

The Hand Axe

It's almost impossible to maintain a bright fire after a week-long rain without a wood-splitting tool of some sort. A big axe is fine if weight is no object and you've got the space to carry it. Otherwise, a high-quality all-steel hand axe will suffice. Despite what you may have read and heard about the dangers of hatchets, they are really quite safe if you follow the guidelines below. When used along with a folding saw, a hand axe will produce all the camp wood you need, with surprisingly little effort.

　　　　　　　　　　B A S I C   E S S E N T I A L S

1. Saw wood to be split into 12-inch lengths.

2. Use the hand axe as a splitting wedge: Do not chop with it! The folding saw performs all cutting functions.

3. Set the axe head lightly into the end grain of the wood (Figure 2-3). One person holds the tool while a friend pounds it through with a chunk of log. All-steel hand axes are better for this than those with wooden handles because they are less likely to break. When splitting very thick (more than 6 inches thick) logs, take multiple splitting off the edges.

Caution. **Hold the axe solidly with both hands. Allow the log hammer to do all the work.**

To produce kindling. Kindling splits easiest from the end grain, a process that's made easier and safer if you use a stick of wood to hold the upright in place (Figure 2-4).

Sharpening the axe. Remove nicks with a flat mill file. True the edge with a diamond stone or soft Arkansas stone. Leave a coating of oil on the blade to resist rust.

Figure 2-3

Splitting wood is easy if you use the axe as a splitting wedge rather than a "chopping" tool. Thick logs can be split by this method (below).

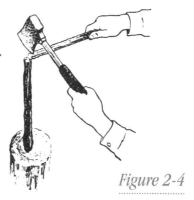

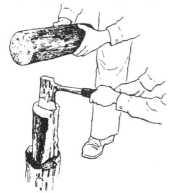

Figure 2-4

Kindling splits easier from the end grain—a process that is made easier (and safer) if you use a stick of wood to hold the upright piece in place (above).

Figure 2-5

The Trailblazer Saw.

20   BASIC ESSENTIALS

Folding Saw

This tool is a must for making fire on a rainy day. Steel-framed bow saws are sturdy (fine for car camping) but they don't pack well. Aluminum-framed folding saws are flimsy, and their triangular shapes don't permit you to cut big logs.

Three excellent trail saws I can recommend are:

The tubular aluminum Trailblazer (Figure 2-5) is a full-stroke rectangular saw in the old bucksaw tradition. It's sized to cut big logs and comes with a wood blade and meat blade (see Appendix).

The Fast Bucksaw. This beautiful hard maple saw (Figure 2-6) has an easily replaced 21-inch blade (refills are available at hardware stores). When assembled, it's so rigid you'd swear it was a one-piece model. Available by mail order from Fast Bucksaw, Inc. (see Appendix).

When it comes to lightweight saws, the **Sawvivor** (Figure 2-6) can't be beat. Its rectangular aluminum frame assembles in seconds and locks tight, with no play what-soever. The saw weighs just 10.5 ounces, complete with a 15-inch blade. Most camping shops have it. The Sawvivor is an official saw of the U.S. Army.

Figure 2-6
....

The Sawvivor (below) and the Fast Bucksaw (right).

To Build a Fire

The ability to make fire when the woods are drenched from rain is one of the most difficult and important of all outdoor tasks. Yet it is a skill which few people possess. Here's how to get the job done quickly and efficiently, regardless of the whims of nature (see Figure 3-1).

Some years ago, after a gentle rain, I watched for an hour while two teenagers tried to build a campfire. The boys struck match after match without success, ultimately giving up in disgust. I casually strolled over, rearranged a few pieces of wood, and with a single match, set the mass aflame.

After witnessing scores of similar episodes, I concluded that while anyone can make fire on a sun-scorched day, precious few have the ability when the weather deteriorates to persistent rain.

Skeptical? Stroll around a state park campground after a tingling thundershower and count the number of fires you see burning brightly compared to the amount of wet gear hanging hopelessly out to dry.

Wilderness guidebooks suggest that a knowledgeable woodsman can start a fire with a single match instantly in a major storm. Hardly! No one can make fire reliably under these conditions, but anyone can succeed in a moderate downpour or weeklong drizzle if he or she knows how.

Know-how begins with the right tinder, and to come up with that, you'll need the right tools—a folding saw, a small hand axe (hatchet), and a sharp knife—hence the importance of the previous chapter.

Now for that tinder. In the north country, the tendency is to search for birchbark—much to the detriment of the birch trees and displeasure of campers who may later occupy the site. Besides, any birchbark you find during or immediately after a good soaking rain is probably too wet to burn anyway. And on a dry day there are better alternatives.

Instead, seek out the dead, pencil-thin branches near the base of evergreen trees. These shade-killed twigs are protected from rain by the tree canopy and are usually bone-dry. They'll break with a crisp snap even after days of prolonged rain. If the branches are wet to the touch but you can hear the snap, the wood's dry enough to burn. A handful of this tinder is all you need.

If evergreen twigs are rain-soaked or unavailable (and in state parks they are *not* available), locate a log with a dry center. Search the open areas of your campsite for a length of jutting birch, pine, cedar, or other softwood. When you find one of these "blowdowns" poking into the clearing, saw off a section that doesn't touch the ground. Touch the cut end to your cheek or lips. The outer sapwood may be damp, but the heartwood should feel dry. Some basic biology here: You'll find deadfalls in the woods as well as in the open, but they're often rotten from the dampness of the forest—and rotten wood, as everyone knows, burns poorly. However, snags that protrude from the forest are flooded with sunlight (which kills most decay-causing microorganisms) and so are more apt to have sound, dry wood inside.

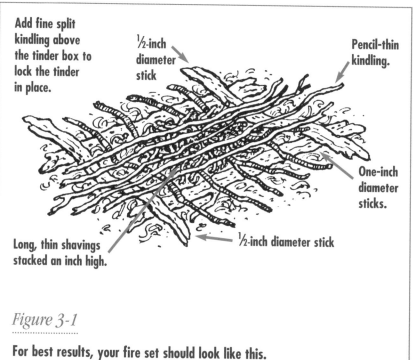

Add fine split kindling above the tinder box to lock the tinder in place.

½-inch diameter stick

Pencil-thin kindling.

One-inch diameter sticks.

½-inch diameter stick

Long, thin shavings stacked an inch high.

Figure 3-1

For best results, your fire set should look like this.

Saw the sun-lit section of log into 12-inch lengths and split and sliver it with the hand axe by the method outlined in Chapter 2. Next, slice long thin slivers of wood from the heartwood splittings. This is your tinder. When you have plenty of tinder on hand, build your fire step-by-step.

Step One

Set two 1-inch diameter sticks parallel to one another about 6 inches apart. Place a few pencil-thin pieces of kindling over them at right angles. Space the pieces of kindling about an inch apart.

Step Two

Carefully place long thin shavings or small dry twigs (tinder) on top of the kindling. Don't crowd the tinder; the fire must have adequate ventilation to burn properly.

Next, put two sticks about ½-inch in diameter over the ends of the inch-thick sticks at right angles to the fire base. These sticks will support the heavier kindling, which you will pile atop the shavings.

Step Three

When you've stacked the shavings about one inch high, weight them in place (so the wind won't blow them away) with several criss-crossed pencil-thin sticks. Follow this with a few larger pieces of wood. For best results, use split kindling rather than sticks gathered from the forest floor.

Your fire is now ready to light. It will start with a single match. The procedure I've outlined is time-consuming but foolproof.

THE UNIQUE CONSTRUCTION OF THE FIRE GUARANTEES SUCCESS BECAUSE:

1. The match is applied directly below the tinder in keeping with the principle that heat (and flame) goes upward, not sideways. Typical campfires are ordinarily ignited along the edge.

2. The tinder box is elevated, which produces an efficient chimney-like draft. The rich, smoke-free flame of the young blaze gains momentum quickly.

3. The tinder doesn't touch the cold, damp ground.

Tips

In the piney woods of the North and East, look for the balsam fir tree. Its sap is nearly as volatile as kerosene. In summer the tree produces half-dollar-size resin blisters on its trunk. Lance a few blisters with a sharp stick and collect the pitch on a piece of wood or bark. Set the "resin cup" directly under your fire base and light it. Voilá! Fire every time—with one match.

Carry a butane lighter and save matches for emergencies. Also bring a candle plus some Fire Ribbon or other chemical fire-starter. For trips where a quick warming fire may be required, assemble these kit materials: A flattened half-gallon milk carton, a handful of thick shavings, and some splittings of scrap wood. Put everything into a nested pair of plastic bags.

When the emergency strikes, dump everything on the ground, frizz up the milk carton, and splash it with Fire Ribbon. Light the ribbon and toss all the wood on top. The carton will burn for about three minutes, the wood an additional five. That's enough time for you to search the woods for more fuel while your wet friend is being re-warmed by your instant blaze.

LET'S REVIEW THE RULES FOR MAKING A SUCCESSFUL FIRE:

1. Place sticks far enough apart on the fire base so there'll be adequate ventilation for the developing flames. The most common reason for fire failure is lack of oxygen.

2. Tinder should be no larger in diameter than the thickness of a match. Trying to ignite wood larger than that on a damp day is a waste of time.

3. Don't heap the fire base high with wood during the developing stages of the flame. Unnecessary fuel just draws heat from the young fire and cools it. Pre-set pyramid-style fires (a la Boy Scouts) look nice in handbooks but burn inefficiently. Once you complete Step 3, wood should be added one stick at a time and placed strategically so you can see light between each one. Smoke is nature's way of telling you you're suffocating the blaze.

Banking the fire to preserve fuel. Use this procedure when you have a good, hot fire but little wood to maintain it. "Bank" your fire by setting small logs parallel to one another across the top. The rule of thumb for a smoke-free flame is to allow a radius width between parallel pieces of wood. Thus, a pair of 2-inch thick logs should be separated by a full inch to ensure adequate ventilation. Banking will reduce this distance to a mere (though identifiable) slit, which will naturally diminish use of oxygen and slow combustion. You should also eliminate any breeze coming into the fire. A large flat rock—don't get one from a lake or river; contained moisture may cause it to explode—or tier of logs works fine.

Extinguishing the blaze. It should go without saying that your fire *must* be dead out when you leave your campsite. The rules are simple: When the smoke is gone and you have thoroughly doused everything with water, check the fire with your hands. If it's hot enough to burn your fingers, it's hot enough to burn a forest.

Choosing a Camp Stove

Y
ou can, of course, cook everything over an open fire. And a lot of campers do just that. But maintaining a cooking fire in the typical state park campground—where wood must be purchased at a dollar a bundle—is comparable to burning money. In the deep backcountry, a stove is less essential, for good wood is readily found. If, however, you've driven many miles to a favorite wilderness and found a fire ban in effect, you'll wish you'd brought a stove.

Summary of Stove Types

There are gasoline, kerosene, propane, butane, alcohol, and wood (twig)-burning stoves. There are also some "multifuel" stoves (see Figure 4-1), which are purported to burn a number of different liquid fuels. These may not put out as much heat as those designed to burn white gas (naptha) only.

Gasoline stoves are the most reliable of the pack, especially in bad weather. And gasoline has the highest heat output of all stove fuels. Generally, gasoline stoves accept only "white" gas or Coleman fuel (highly refined forms of naptha). It's not safe to burn leaded gasoline in them. An important distinction must be made between additive-free white gasoline—which is difficult to obtain—and additive-packed automotive unleaded gasoline, which is available at every gas station. Unleaded gas is more volatile than white gas and may produce excessive pressures in stoves designed for white gas only.

Kerosene has about the same BTU rating as gasoline, but it's less volatile. Where a gasoline stove will explode, a kerosene stove will simply burn. But kerosene stoves are smelly, and they must be primed

Figure 4-1

A multifuel stove.

with alcohol or gasoline. Nonetheless, they are very safe and are grand for camp cooking.

Propane is relatively inexpensive and it puts out good heat. Its big drawback is in the packaging: The heavy steel cylinders that contain the gas are fine in a Vanbago but not in the packsack of a hiker or canoeist.

Butane stoves are cutesy affairs that light with the turn of an adjuster knob. They need no pumping, priming, or filling. Refueling takes seconds and consists of merely snapping on a new gas cylinder. But butane stoves put out little heat: The colder it gets the less flame they manage. At around freezing, they quit working altogether. You won't find experienced campers using butane stoves. They're fine for high-altitude work where the gas develops sufficient pressure. But for all-around camping, there are better alternatives.

Blended fuels. Some manufacturers blend butane and propane for better cold-weather performance; however, their heat output is still well below that of stoves that burn white gas.

Alcohol stoves are safe and reliable. Just light the burner and you're ready to cook. Alcohol stoves are slow to heat, however. Most require ten to fifteen minutes to boil a quart of water! **Sterno** is a solid form of alcohol that comes in a can. Sterno puts out enough heat to warm food but not cook it.

Wood-burning stoves. If you like campfires, you'll love wood-burning stoves. Woodstoves are lightweight and powerful, and the twigs they burn are free. But the wood burns fast, so you'll have to keep fueling the stove as you cook. The **Super Sierra** stove (figure 4-2) has a battery-operated fan and damper to control the temperature. It puts out 15,000 BTUs—twice that of most gasoline stoves! The Super Sierra performs well in any weather, even with damp wood. I use mine to start fires on rainy days and to burn garbage when I'm camping above the treeline, where the only fuel available is small sticks. The Super Sierra is available from Z.Z. Corporation (see Appendix).

Figure 4-2

Super Sierra (Zip!) Stove.

It runs on an AA battery and burns almost anything.

Stove Features

Stability. There's nothing more frustrating than simmering a big pot of spaghetti on a precarious little beast that wobbles with every stir of the spoon. Before you buy, remember that some stoves that look great in the store tip over in the field.

Ease of starting. Stoves that come equipped with built-in pumps start faster and generally put out more heat than those without pumps. For general camping, a pump is a must.

Susceptibility to wind. The first time you have to build a rock wall around your stove to keep it perking you'll understand the value of a good windscreen. Avoid stoves with thin aluminum windscreens that burn up, or detachable ones that can be lost.

Adjustable flame. If you intend to fry pancakes or simmer stew, you'll want an infinitely adjustable flame—a feature most compact trail stoves don't have. The venerable Coleman twin burner and compact PEAK 1 offer the finest adjustments of any stoves currently available.

Plastic parts. Plastic is bad medicine for stove parts. Plastic hardens with heat and age and eventually breaks. If there's a stove flare-up, plastic will melt and burn. Also stay away from any stove that does not have a flameproof armored fuel line.

Here are some do's and don'ts that will keep your camp stove perking merrily season after season.

Do's

◆ **Do carry fuel only in recommended containers.** Volatiles are best transported in aluminum liter bottles or in the original steel can.

◆ **Do frequently check the temperature** of your stove's fuel tank by feeling it with your hand. If the tank is too hot to hold, reduce the stove's heat and/or pour cold water on the tank.

◆ **Do carry extra stove parts and tools.** An extra pressure cap and leather pump washer is usually enough. Bring a small screwdriver and pliers.

◆ **Do empty the fuel** in your stove at the end of each season. Impurities in fuel left in stoves can cause malfunctions. **Note: This is the most common cause of long-term stove failure.**

Don'ts

◆ **Don't loosen or remove the filler cap** of a gasoline stove when the stove is burning. This could result in an explosion.

◆ **Don't re-fuel a hot stove.** There may be sufficient heat still available to ignite the gas fumes.

◆ **Don't set oversize pots on stoves.** Large pots reflect excessive heat back to the fuel tank, which may cause overheating of the stove. Run stoves at three-fourths of maximum heat output if you use oversize pots.

◆ **Don't use automotive gasoline** (regular or unleaded) in a stove designed to burn white gas.

◆ **Don't start a stove inside a tent** or confined area; the resulting flare-up can be dangerous.

◆ **Don't operate any stove without sufficient ventilation.** A closed tent is not sufficiently ventilated.

◆ **Don't set stoves on sleeping bags** or tent floors. There's enough heat generated at the base of some stoves to melt or warp these items.

◆ **Don't run stoves at full power** for extended periods of time. The tank may overheat and cause the safety valve to blow.

◆ **Don't enclose a stove with aluminum foil** to increase its heat output. The stove may overheat and explode.

◆ **Don't fill gasoline or kerosene stoves** more than three-fourths full. Fuel won't vaporize if there's insufficient room for it to expand.

Tasty Routes to Dining Out

There are two schools of thought about camp cooking: One prefers spending whatever time is required to make delicious meals, even if it means sweating for hours over a smoky fire and dutch oven. The other view goes something like this: "Since I spend only about a week a year in the outdoors, I like to keep foods simple. If it takes more than twenty minutes to prepare, forget it."

I prefer the latter approach, as the following example illustrates: Some years ago, after a gentle rain, I went for an evening paddle along the shore of a popular lake in the Boundary Waters Canoe Area. As I rounded a point, I happened upon a man and woman sitting contentedly on a rock ledge, staring into the starlit sky. I paddled over and struck up a conversation, in the course of which I asked: "How come you folks don't have a bright, cheery fire going?"

With this, the man began his story. He and his wife were newcomers to the backcountry—neither had canoed or camped before. They arranged to have an outfitter supply all their needs, and he reciprocated by providing a wealth of slow-cook foods. There were pancakes and French toast for breakfast, grilled cheese sandwiches and soup for lunch, and multi-course dried foods for supper—all of which required a well-maintained fire or stove (which the couple didn't have) to prepare.

"For the first three days we followed the menu," said the man. "We got up early and built our cooking fire; stopped at noon and built another. It was a hassle. By the end of the third day we had covered only 15 miles. Then the rains hit and we couldn't start a fire. So we pulled out all the dried stuff—crackers and cheese, peanut butter and jelly, etc. With no fires to slow us down, we began making time. We started averaging 15 miles a day instead of 5. Now, we're seeing the country—and that's what we came here for!"

When I offered to show the couple how to make a wet-weather fire, they politely declined, reaffirming their commitment to the joys of efficient traveling.

Admittedly, PBJ's and cold cheese sandwiches are not my cup of tea, even on a fast-paced camping trip. I prefer a more middle-ground approach—a reasonably quick breakfast, no-cook lunch, and a lazy but determined supper. Some of my favorite trail meals are listed below:

Easy Breakfasts

When cold granola and instant oatmeal get boring, try these delicious hot cereals:

Red River Cereal is a nutritious blend of crunchy grains that's served in the best fishing camps in Canada. It cooks to a rich creamy consistency in just five minutes. Most supermarkets have it.

Kashi is a breakfast pilaf made from seven whole grains and sesame. It's a pleasant change from traditional hot cereals.

Sturdiwheat hot cereal has a rich taste (the outer wheat layers are left on the grain). Get it from the Sturdiwheat company in Red Wing, Minnesota (see Appendix).

Old time, slow-cook oatmeal. Really, now, when did you last have the real thing?

If you want to make these cereals taste grand, add dehydrated fruit, raisins, and brown sugar to the cold water before you start cooking. For mouth-watering elegance, include chopped dates and walnuts.

No cereal is complete without milk, which you'll have to rehydrate from powdered form. Most powdered milk you find in grocery stores tastes awful. *Milkman* ("with the kiss of cream") is by far the best. It's available only in camping stores. *Sanalac*, which you'll find at specialty supermarkets, is nearly as good and much less expensive.

Lunches

Except when I operate out of a base camp, I prefer lunches that need no cooking. My meals tend to be nutritious but spartan, and center around these ingredients:

Pita (Mediterranean pocket) bread—keeps at least a week without
 refrigeration
Assorted cheeses and hard sausage
Granola bars

Peanut butter and jelly
Wylers or Kool-Aid instant fruit drink
Hard candies
Something salty—mixed nuts, pretzels, etc.

Suppers

After two very predictable meals, supper is a blessing. Often I am quite extravagant, relying on canned sauces and fresh vegetables to spark life into the menu. Instant Lipton and Knorr soups are a traditional part of every dinner, as is some kind of dessert. If time permits, I'll bake cinnamon rolls or chocolate cake on my trail stove (see section on ovens, page 37), and later contentedly pig out on popcorn and spiced tea. Otherwise, I rely on dried foods such as Minute Rice, instant mashed potatoes, noodles, and Bisquick. And for auto camping, where weight is no object, anything goes—that is, if it will fit in my sixty-quart ice chest.

Go-light campers may find that one-pot meals get boring in a few days. Midway through a long trip, I serve Pita Pizza: It's everyone's favorite meal.

Pita Pizza for Four

INGREDIENTS

One or two pieces of pita bread per person

½ cup dried tomato powder or 1 14-ounce can of tomato paste

⅓ lb. Fresh mozzarella cheese (vacuum-sealed cheese keeps for weeks)

Spices: oregano, garlic powder, salt, cayenne pepper, basil

Suggested toppings: pepperoni, summer sausage, hard salami, fresh onion, black olives, canned mushrooms, anchovies, smoked oysters, etc.

PROCEDURE

1. Slice and fry the meat and drain off the grease on paper toweling. Thickly dice the vegetables and mushrooms, fry them in light oil, then drain off the grease and set them aside.

2. To make the pizza sauce, pour the tomato powder into a bowl and add water to make a thick paste, or use canned tomato paste. Sprinkle on oregano, garlic, basil, salt, and cayenne.

3. Fry an unsliced pita at low heat in a well-oiled (I prefer olive oil), covered skillet. When the bottom of the pita is brown (in about twenty seconds), flip it over and thickly spread on tomato sauce, cheese, cooked meat, and toppings to taste. Immediately add a dash of water (to steam-melt the cheese) and cover the pan. Allow the pizza to cook at very low heat for half a minute, or until the cheese has melted. You'll love it.

Munchies

Car campers will prey heavily on junk foods, while hikers, bikers and canoeists will opt for more nutritious snacks, such as fruitcake, dehydrated fruit, popcorn, granola bars, and mixed nuts. (Note: Cashews have the highest nutritional value of the various nuts.)

Packing Suggestions

To eliminate confusion, package each meal for your group as a complete unit. Remove all unnecessary packaging to save as much weight and space as possible. I pack flowable solids such as Tang and baking mix in small Ziploc bags, which are then encased in sturdy nylon bags. Breakable and crushable items such as crackers and cheese go inside rigid cardboard containers. A cut-down cereal box works fine, but a half-gallon milk carton is ideal. Later, in camp, you can use the milk carton for mixing Kool-Aid and puddings. Or shred it up for use as an emergency fire-starter.

Each plastic-bagged meal should be placed into its own color-coded waterproof nylon sack. You'll save much pack groping at meal time if you adopt a color-coded system. I traditionally pack my breakfasts in green bags, my lunches in blue, and suppers in red. Since I don't like surprises, I label the contents of each sack on the outside with crayon.

If you pack your food in discreet, pre-measured units as I suggest, everything will be at hand—and you'll never have to eat damp oatmeal.

Liquids are best carried in plastic bottles which have screw-cap lids. Nalgene polyethylene containers (see Figure 5-1) are the most reliable, although they are expensive. Supermarket syrup and honey bottles work marginally well if you replace their plastic pop-tops with rigid caps that won't accidentally release. Another solution is to melt the flip tops to a mass of flowable plastic in the burner of your stove.

Hospitals and clinics throw away plastic "sterile water for irrigation" bottles after a single use. These marginally flexible bottles

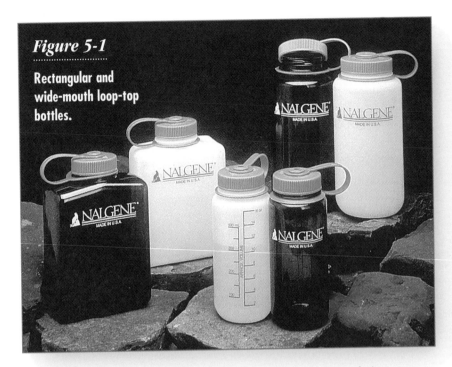

Figure 5-1

Rectangular and
wide-mouth loop-top
bottles.

range in size from 500 to 1500 mL and have raised mL gradations on
one side. Sterile water bottles are surprisingly strong and won't hold
odors like other containers made from more porous plastics. They
have a gasketed screw cap on top and a folding plastic "lanyard" ring
(to hang them upside down) on the bottom. They come filled with
sterile water, so they're more germ-free than any container you can
buy. Ask your local hospital to save some of these marvelous plastic
bottles for you.

Food Preparation Hints

Biscuits and cakes. Don't mix batter in a bowl: It's too messy.
Instead, pre-measure the bake-stuff into a large plastic bag. Add water
to the bag then knead its contents until the texture is right. Cut a slit
in the bag bottom then squeeze (use the bag like a cake decorator)
the contents into your awaiting oven. Voilà! No mess or waste. Burn
the plastic bag.

Making popcorn. Making popcorn for large groups is a hassle,
even if you have a large pot. Here's an easier way: As you complete
each batch of popped corn, pour it into a large paper grocery sack
(don't use a plastic bag—the hot corn will melt through it!). Season
the corn and shake the bag to mix. Later, burn the bag.

Paper towels. Paper toweling is always handy on a campout. If you pack a half-dozen sheets of toweling with each meal, you won't have to search for the main roll when dishwashing time rolls around.

Cookware

You can get along with about half as much cookware as you think you need. Two nesting pots, a coffee pot, fry pan, plastic bowls, insulated cups, and spoons are sufficient for a party of four.

Don't waste your money on Trail Queen nested cooksets that contain useless items. Buy the pots you need and fill out the rest with materials from your kitchen. In the end you'll save weight, space, and money, and enjoy real utility.

Ovens

If you plan to bake, you'll need an oven of some sort. Polished aluminum reflector ovens are traditional but outdated in these days of small fires and trail stoves. My vote goes to the Jell-O mold oven (Figure 5-2), which is nothing more than a large ring aluminum Jell-O mold and a high cover. Jell-O mold ovens will work on any trail stove and will produce quality bake stuff in about the same time as your home oven.

TO USE THE JELL-O MOLD FOR BAKING ON YOUR STOVE:

1. Grease the mold and pour your bake stuff into the outside ring. Decrease the suggested amount of water by up to one fourth for faster baking.

2. Bring the stove to its normal operating temperature, then reduce the heat to the lowest possible blue-flame setting. Center the Jell-O mold over the burner head, top it with a high cover (necessary to provide sufficient room for the bake goods to rise), and relax. Cooking times are nearly identical to those suggested in the baking directions.

Figure 5-2

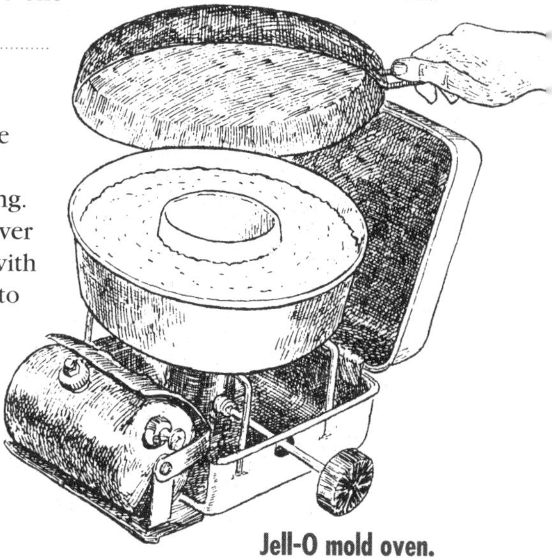

Jell-O mold oven.

Tip. **"Large burner" stoves such as the Coleman Peak 1 and double-burner models, may burn the edges of the bake stuff. An electric stove burner shield—available for a few dollars at most supermarkets—will eliminate this problem. Simply place the shield under the Jell-O mold. The air space between the shield and mold bottom will prevent burning. The large-size burner shield will fit large-ring Jell-O molds perfectly.**

The triple-pan method of baking on your stove is another alternative. You'll need two nesting skillets, a high cover, and a half dozen small nails or stones.

1. Evenly scatter the nails or stones onto the surface of the large (bottom) frying pan.

2. Place your bake stuff into the small frying pan and set it on top of the nails or stones (the two pans must be separated by nails or stones to prevent burning).

3. Cover the unit and place it on your stove. Use the lowest possible blue-flame setting.

Warning: **Don't use this method with a thin aluminum skillet on the bottom; you'll burn a hole right through it!**

Pitfalls of Winter Cooking

Your body burns much more energy in winter than in summer, so rely heavily on foods which are rich in fat and carbohydrates (fats contain about twice as many calories per pound as carbohydrates and are the body's major source of stored energy). Unfortunately, some fat-rich foods that are summer favorites don't work well in winter. A good example is peanut butter. Try chiseling peanut butter out of a poly bottle at twenty below zero and you'll see why.

Cheese, another high-fat food, doesn't fare too well either—mainly because it tastes like candle wax when near frozen. However, cheese melts nicely into any hot food.

Salami (any sausage) on the other hand, tastes good frozen or thawed. You can use it as is or to fortify soups and freeze-dried entrees.

Food preparation tips. It takes much longer to cook foods in winter than in summer, so increase cooking times substantially. "Cook-in-the-bag" entrees such as those made by Mountain House will cook at low temperatures if you set the boiling water–filled food bag into a covered pot of near boiling water for ten minutes. This procedure will assure complete cooking and eliminate a dirty pot.

Since an icy wind can rob heat from a thin aluminum pot almost as fast as your stove can produce it, keep your pots covered and sheltered. A good procedure is to simply burrow the kitchen below the surface of the snow. You may also want to make a cozy for your pots from any quilted or knitted material. A two-piece cozy (top hat and Velcro-secured band) is more versatile and energy efficient than a one-piece "teapot" model. When your food has cooked, remove the pot from the flame, set it on a square of closed-cell foam, and slip on the cozy. Use spare clothing (not nylon, which melts!) for insulation if you don't have "proper" cozies.

Washing dishes. Some winter campers advise cleaning dishes with snow (a messy procedure). I've found it's better to wash them the traditional way in boiling water (no soap). I wear light wool gloves under plastic-coated cotton ones to keep my hands toasty warm and dry throughout the experience. Bacteria are inactive in frigid temperatures, so it's not necessary to rinse and dry your cookware. A little grease on your bowl won't hurt you—as long as it's *your* grease. It follows that each camper must have his/her own bowl, cup, and spoon.

Bowls and such. Give some thought to the selection of plastic cups and bowls. Plastic that is brittle in the store may shatter on the winter trail. Surprisingly, inexpensive, flexible plastics are often superior to stronger but more brittle, expensive ones.

Keep your cooking and eating utensils secured in a compartmented fabric roll so you won't lose them in a snowdrift. And pack spices in film containers, not salt shakers which gum up.

Cold feet. The cook spends considerable time just standing around, so some sort of insulation underfoot is essential. An 18-inch square of half-inch-thick closed-cell foam is ideal. I suggest you don't use your foam sleeping pad for this purpose, because your nighttime comfort depends on keeping it absolutely dry.

To light up your life. Winter days are short, so you may need to depend on artificial light for cooking. Flashlights are generally unsuitable in subzero temperatures, and candle lanterns don't produce enough light. Your best bet is a miner's headlamp (the type that takes four D cells). If you use alkaline batteries and keep the battery pack inside your parka for warmth, you'll have enough light to last a week on the typical cross-country ski trip.

To keep liquids from freezing. Liquids freeze less rapidly if they're capped and submerged in the snow. Freezing begins at the air interface of a liquid, so store beverage-filled poly bottles *upside* *down.* This way you're less apt to experience the difficulty of removing a frozen bottle cap.

A Thermos bottle may save more than its weight in stove fuel. I fill my Thermos as soon as the tea is done to save reheating it later. If there's a campfire, I set the Thermos near it for warmth. And when I retire, the vacuum bottle goes into the bag with me to ensure a ready hot drink come morning.

Major cooking dangers. When it's twenty below and you're dressed in a down parka and double-shell mittens, performing simple chores such as turning down the stove or lifting a pot cover takes on new dimensions. A real danger centers around use of the stove. For example, I once burned a large hold in the sleeve of an expensive down parka when I passed my arm too close to the stove burner. Subzero clothing is a good insulator, so you may not detect a burn until much of your outfit has gone up in flames. Be extremely careful around stoves when you're bundled up.

Incidentally, use care when handling stove fuels (gasoline and kerosene) in cold weather. Liquid fuels freeze at much lower temperatures than water so you're set for instant frostbite should you inadvertently spill some on bare hands. For safety sake, handle fuel bottles while wearing gloves.

Leftovers. A major summer problem—what to do with uneaten food—is minimized in winter. I simply scoop frozen food waste into a Ziploc bag and carry it along until I have the opportunity to burn it. Some winter travelers leave uneaten food on the snow for the animals—a practice not approved by national park and forest service personnel. Careless food habits—especially in winter when natural foods are scarce—might turn an ordinarily shy critter into a bold, nasty one. Wild animals are perfectly capable of finding their own dinner (in any season) without man's help.

Old hands at summer camping should have no trouble adapting to the subtle differences of the winter kitchen. The important thing is to experiment with foods and cooking procedures *before* you take to the winter woods.

Expert Camping Procedures

For two days, the TV blasted warnings of the coming storm. Just south of us were 40-mile-an-hour winds and ice-cold rain. By all reports, the weather system would hit us sometime Saturday. Nonetheless, we refused to alter our plans, the rule in Scouting being "You never cancel a campout."

When we pulled into the campground, the sky was already darkening. Scoutmaster Chic Sheridan and I studied the terrain: We figured we had maybe an hour to rig a snug camp, so we went to work immediately.

There were three spots for tents: The lower level—located about 2 feet above the river, would provide room for a half dozen tents. The wide flat terrace farther up could take four. And the gentle rolling hill top could hold two or three.

An upward glance revealed that the hill was out of the question, as it was already occupied by a state-of-the-art nylon dome. Granted, we could probably crowd one or two Scout tents along side, but the positioning would be only temporary: The first story blast would send them crashing down. No, the hill was simply a bad location.

On the lower level near the river, there was plenty of space for our five tents, but we declined the option, knowing full well the dangers of a major storm and a rising river.

"Over there," called Chic, pointing to the center terrace. "Get 'em up boys!" Now, the apparent disorder of before came to a halt. Suddenly, everyone seemed to know exactly what he was doing. Within minutes, tents were pitched and battened for the worst.

The Scout tents were primitive compared to the exotic dome on the hill—just old but solid canvas wall tents with sewn-in floors and a

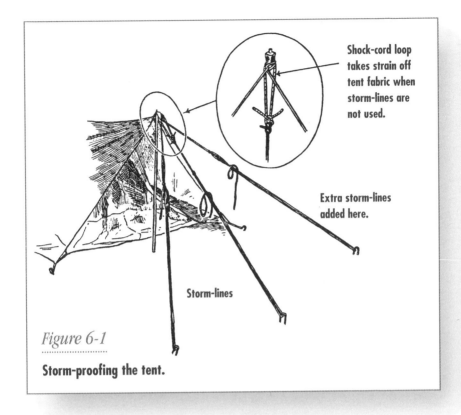

Shock-cord loop takes strain off tent fabric when storm-lines are not used.

Extra storm-lines added here.

Storm-lines

Figure 6-1

Storm-proofing the tent.

single vertical pole at each end. Nonetheless, we knew they'd withstand quite a blow if properly rigged.

First, the boys placed on oversize 4-mil plastic groundsheet inside each tent, taking care to fold the edges of the plastic well up the sidewalls. This would protect the sleeping bags of those boys who slept along the perimeter. Next, they attached two stout guylines to each tent peak (Figure 6-1) and fanned them out to stakes below. Each tent was now held firm by three taut ropes at each end. Years before, I had installed loops of quarter-inch shock cord at the peak of each tent to absorb the stress normally reserved for the stitching and fabric.

"Run storm lines off the side, too! And weight the windward stakes with big rocks," I called. The younger Scouts followed the example of the older ones, who scampered about and barked commands. The boys meticulously tied lengths of parachute cord to the nylon loops we'd sewn to the tent hems. Now, instead of just three stakes per sidewall, there were five. The view from the hill looked like Charlotte's web. Hopefully, it would be as secure.

"Okay, boys," I shouted. "Let's get two rain flies (tarps) up. Pair 'em off a common ridge. Get on it!"

Again, the fir began to fly. First, a drum-tight rope was strung between two trees. Then two boys tied the ridge of the tarp while two more staked the tail. Coiled loops of parachute cord tied to the main face of the tarp were pulled free and staked out to nearby trees (Figure 6-2)—a procedure that required less than three minutes. When the first fly was set, a second was mated, A-frame fashion, along side. No need to search for extra cord or stakes—everything required was in the nylon bag that contained each tarp (see Rigging The Tarp, page 47).

Ten minutes later we crowded under the low-slung flies, ready to prepare a gourmet supper and laugh at the whims of nature. I fired up the big Optimus 111B stove and put on the coffeepot while Chic greeted the three college kids who'd dropped in to comment on our show.

"That your dome up there?" I questioned, pointing to the hill.

"Yeah," said one of the boys proudly.

"You know you're right in the path of the storm," I quipped.

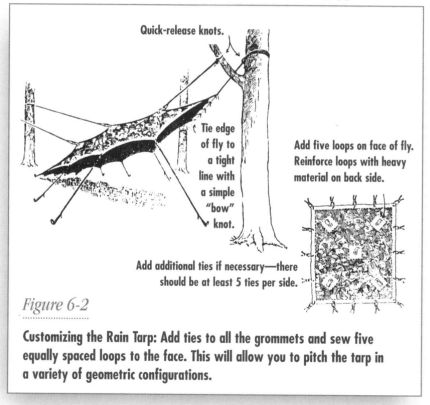

Quick-release knots.

Tie edge of fly to a tight line with a simple "bow" knot.

Add five loops on face of fly. Reinforce loops with heavy material on back side.

Add additional ties if necessary—there should be at least 5 ties per side.

Figure 6-2

Customizing the Rain Tarp: Add ties to all the grommets and sew five equally spaced loops to the face. This will allow you to pitch the tarp in a variety of geometric configurations.

"No biggie," was the reply. "They say it'll take 50-mile-an-hour winds."

"Hope you're right: The test will come any time now."

With that, one of the boys poked gentle fun at our canvas menagerie, slyly suggesting that the wind gods would probably flatten everything by morning. I just smiled: We knew better.

Within the hour it began, innocently at first, with a light drizzle that lasted for an hour. Then the storm intensified; soon rain fell in thick sheets, driven by winds of 40 miles an hour.

Once during the night I sat up in despair and hugged the rear pole, certain the tent was about to come crashing down. But it held fast, testimony to our weatherproofing.

We awoke the following morning to the scene of disaster. There were downed trees and debris everywhere. One of our tents was partially collapsed, though the boys inside were still fast asleep. I stole a skyward glance toward the hilltop. The dome? It was gone, and so were the boys who'd occupied it. All that remained was a swatch of blue nylon tangled in branches high above.

Chic and I exchanged smug glances: We'd weathered the storm!

LET'S REVIEW THE PROCEDURES FOR EFFECTIVE STORMPROOFING:

1. Always use a plastic groundcloth inside your tent. Water that wicks through worn floor fabric and/or seams will be trapped by the ground sheet. Never put the groundcloth under the tent floor.

2. Attach loops of shock cord or bands cut from inner tubes to all guylines. Shock cords take up the wind stress normally reserved for seams and fittings. Even a badly sewn, poorly reinforced tent can be used in severe weather if it's outfitted with shock cords.

3. Know the shortcomings of your tent and correct them. Reinforce questionable seams and add additional stake loops if you need them.

4. When high winds threaten, run additional guylines off each tent peak.

Special considerations for stormproofing self-supporting tents

Most of today's tents are somewhat self-supporting, such as the Eureka! Timberline, and most domes. This can be good or bad, depending on how seriously you take the "self-supporting" part. The fact is, you *must* stake and guy self-supporting tents or they'll blow down in big winds. It can be very entertaining to watch a cheap dome tent in a high wind—an oncoming gust flattens the tent, which seconds later springs back into shape. Unfortunately, those who are sleeping inside aren't laughing.

Domes are very comfortable tents (you can sleep in any direction), but most are poorly ventilated and questionably watertight in heavy rains. They also have lots of long poles, which must be clipped to the canopy or painstakingly threaded through sleeves. And while you're doing this, the tent—which is laying flat on the ground—is exposed to rain. You get exactly what you pay for when you buy a dome tent. Cheap domes leak in rain and blow down in wind; pricey geodesic styles such as the Arctic-proven North Face VE 24-25 are watertight and secure in gale force winds. They are quite remarkable all-weather tents.

USE THESE TRICKS TO STORMPROOF YOUR SELF-SUPPORTING TENT:

1. Sew nylon "storm loops" on the face of the fly, in line with tent poles. Position loops midway down the poles as illustrated in Figure 6-3, and be sure to back what you sew with heavy material. Next, sew a Velcro tab to the inside of

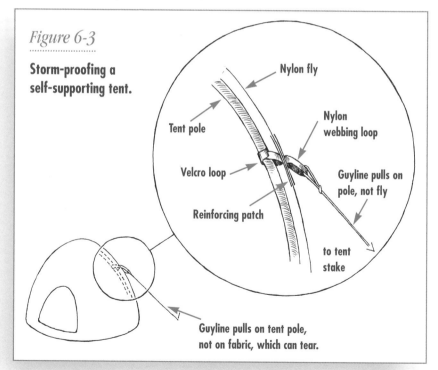

Figure 6-3

Storm-proofing a self-supporting tent.

Nylon fly

Tent pole

Nylon webbing loop

Velcro loop

Guyline pulls on pole, not fly

Reinforcing patch

to tent stake

Guyline pulls on tent pole, not on fabric, which can tear.

the fly, opposite each loop. Seal the seams you've sewn. I prefer to use Thompson's Water Seal, which you can get at any hardware store. One application with a foam varnish brush lasts for years.

When a wind blows up, Velcro the loops to the poles behind them, and run a guyline from the loop to the ground. This will transfer wind stress from the nylon fly directly to the poles. You need to guy only the windward poles.

2. Double-stake your tent on soft ground; use log or rock anchors on rock (figure 6-4). Two stakes per loop—each through a separate hole, and at a different angle—doubles the surface area and holding power in soft ground. On rock or sand, try the method illustrated in figure 6-3.

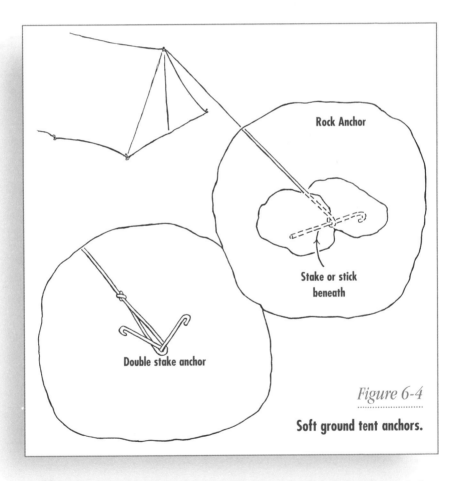

Rock Anchor

Stake or stick beneath

Double stake anchor

Figure 6-4

Soft ground tent anchors.

Tip. **Tie 3-foot lengths of parachute cord to each stake loop before your trip, and you won't have to mess with cutting and tying these anchor lines in a rainstorm!**

3. Buy a vestibule for your tent if one is available: It will completely cover the poorly protected entryway and provide a place to store gear.

4. It bears repeating that you should always use a generously sized plastic groundcloth inside your tent. In winter you may put the groundcloth under your tent to keep the tent floor from freezing to the ground.

Rigging the Tarp

Stormproofing your tent is only half the solution to keeping dry in rain. The other part is having a dry place to cook and relax. A large (10 foot by 12 foot) nylon tarp pitched between trees or suspended from guyed poles will provide ample protection for four.

FOR A QUICK RAINPROOF SHELTER THAT WON'T FLAP IN THE WIND, TRY THIS RIGGING PROCEDURE:

1. String a tight line about 6 feet high between two trees. Use two half-hitches at one end of the rope and a power-cinch with a quick-release knot at the other (see Chapter 7 for a review of knots and hitches).

2. Tie one edge of the fly to the line. This will distribute the wind load among several points along the fly. Wrap the corner ties around the line a few times before you tie them to produce friction so the fly won't slide inward along the line when it's buffeted by wind.

3. Stake down the back end of the fly, then guy the center to an overhanging limb or rope strung overhead. If this is impossible, prop out the center from the inside with a pole. Don't try this unless you've sewn a protective pole patch to the fly. Without one, you'll stretch the fly out of shape or tear it. And don't use Visklamps (ball and garter devices) to pitch a fly. Visklamps stretch and abrade fabric unmercifully.

If the center pole falls down in high winds, the fly will collapse. To secure the pole to the fly, sew two opposing "butterfly pole" loops to the inside of the fly, as illustrated in figure 6-5. Thread a piece of parachute cord through the loops and secure the cords with a nylon cord-lock. Now your center pole will stay put in high winds.

Camping   **47**

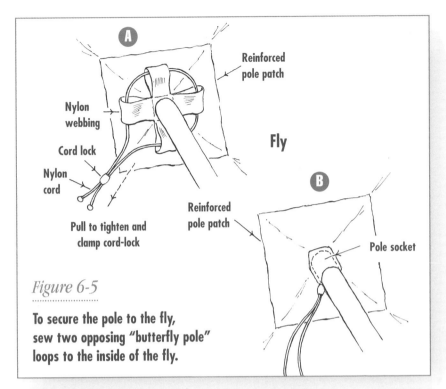

Figure 6-5
....

To secure the pole to the fly, sew two opposing "butterfly pole" loops to the inside of the fly.

To use the "butterfly pole" loops, center the pole in the "socket" and tighten the cord-lock. The loops will wrap around the pole and hold it in place when the tarp is buffeted by wind. For extra security, wrap the cords around the pole a few times and tie them with a simple bow.

4. Guy the sides as the terrain permits. Be sure you complete all knots and hitches with quick-release loops, as explained in Chapter 7, so you can change or drop the outfit at a moment's notice. When severe winds threaten, simply lower one or both ends of the ridge rope.

Packing the fly. Pack your fly in a nylon bag, along with 60 feet of parachute cord (cut into 15-foot lengths) and a half dozen wire tent stakes. This will greatly simplify pitching.

For large groups, pair two tarps at the ridge. Overlap one tarp so there'll be no leaks.

When all-day rains come to stay, it may be necessary to move the campfire under the fly—a procedure that requires raising the tail hem a foot off the ground to provide flow-through ventilation. Without this ventilation you'll do a smoke dance inside. Raising the hem necessarily requires unstaking the fly and meticulously guying each point to distant trees.

Snug Camp

Campcraft books are rich with advice on choosing the right campsite. But most commentary is a waste of space, since even a rank novice knows better than to pitch his tent in a depression, on unlevel ground, or in a bog. Since it's unethical (and often illegal) to clear trees and brush and to "improve" sites by trenching around tents, you usually have to take what's available and make the best of it. Forest Service and Park personnel don't always establish campsites with an eye for the lay of the land. Most of the time, I'm overjoyed just to find a level place to set my tent. After that I worry about creature comforts such as a south facing slope, proximity to good water, effective drainage, shade and wind protection, a nice view, etc.

Nonetheless, here's one bit of advice worth repeating: Don't camp in a meadow or flat mossy area. Cold, damp air settles in meadows, and moss acts like a giant sponge: It traps water for miles around. If it rains while you're camped on moss, you'll be elbow-deep in water by morning. Even the most watertight groundcloth won't save you under these conditions.

Bears

There are two views about bears: One suggests that all bruins are timid and will run at the first smell of you. The other warns that bears are mankillers and advises you to bring big guns.

Between these extremes is the real truth. Most bears are timid and will ordinarily stay away from humans. But bears can be ornery, like some people. Many bears start each new day looking for a meal; if you come upon a recent kill or get between a sow and her cubs, you've got big problems. New research by Stephen Herrero and James Gary Shelton suggest that people may have more to fear from bears than was previously thought. If you're intrigued by bears, read the books *Bear Attacks, Their Causes and Avoidance*, by Stephen Herrero, Lyons and Burford, 1985; *Bear Encounter Survival Guide*, by James Gary Shelton, published by James Gary Shelton, 1994; *Bear Attacks: The Deadly Truth*, by James Gary Shelton, 1998. I suggest you read these books in the order they are listed.

Protecting Your Food Supply

Don't store food inside your car. Bears are experts at getting into cars. They'll insert their claws through the tiniest openings in windows and doors and rip out the glass or metal to get at food. Today's hardtop cars make it relatively easy for a determined bruin to steal food. For this reason, a car is not the best place to store your food.

Use a critter-proof container. A plastic or metal ice chest or thick-walled PVC plastic pipe with threaded end caps will deter ravaging raccoons and ground squirrels. Squirrels have very sharp teeth and will bore right through a nylon packsack. There are some commercial bear-proof containers, but they are heavy, bulky and expensive. If you want to know the current technology, check with the managers of national parks that have a large bear population, such as Yellowstone and Glacier.

Don't hang your food in a tree. Expert campers usually *do not* store their food in trees. Instead, they seal their food tightly in plastic to eliminate odors (I suggest vacuum sealing), then they remove the food from the immediate camp area. Setting food packs outside the campsite perimeter is usually enough to foil hungry bruins and other animals. Rationale: Bears are creatures of habit—they quickly learn that camps, packs, and tin cans contain food. In each campsite there are only a few trees with limbs high enough to deter a bruin. Bears aren't stupid; they learn the location of these trees and make daily rounds to secure whatever is suspended from them. When they find something (anything) hanging from "their" tree, they'll get it down, one way or another. All black bears (even fat old sows) can climb to some degree. And cubs shinny like monkeys. James Gary Shelton has discovered that, contrary to popular belief, grizzlies *can* "hook" climb with their legs, just like humans. The point is that, if momma can't get your food, the kids will! Polar bears are the only bears that absolutely, positively don't climb.

Recommendation. Double-bag (in plastic) all foodstuffs, especially meats. Ask your grocer to vacuum-seal smelly foods. Set food packs on low ground (to minimize the travel of odors) well away from the confines of campsites and trails. As an added precaution, separate food packs by 50 feet or more. Do *not*, as commonly advised, put food packs in trees.

If you're camping in grizzly country, locate your kitchen at least 50 yards downwind of your tents. Naturally, cooking areas must be scrupulously clean—free of even the last Rice Krispy. Nonetheless, human odor is stronger than most food smells: Don't be surprised if the bear smells you before he smells your food.

Bear Encounters

Here are the recommended procedures in the event you meet a bear face to face.

Black Bears

Blackies are timid and will ordinarily run away at the first smell of you. Bears don't see very well; what most people interpret as a "charge" is usually nothing more than simple curiosity. Screaming, blowing whistles, and other noise-making will usually send a wild bear running, but an experienced camp bear will remain totally oblivious to the racket. The best procedure is to hold your ground, spread your arms wide (so you look bigger), talk authoritatively, and back off slowly. *Do not run.* The danger signs are "woofing and clacking." If the bear goes "woof, woof, woof," and you hear loud hiccuping sounds with the clacking of teeth, the situation is deteriorating. The bear's mad and unpredictable. If there's a tree handy, climb it now. If you can beat a path to safer ground, go for it. If you are attacked, fight like mad. Do *not* play dead with a black bear.

Pepper spray (sometimes called "bear mace"), contains 10 percent oleo capsicum, the flaming ingredient in red pepper. If properly used it will stop bears about 75 percent of the time. Herrero did not find a single case where spraying a bear with pepper enraged it and made it more aggressive.

Don't spray your camp to keep bears away. Recent studies suggest that while bears don't like to be sprayed with pepper, they do like the taste of it. Evidently, bears like spicy food, too.

There are a number of formulations of "bear mace." I rely on *Counter Assault*. It's available from Bushwacker Backpack and Supply Company (see Appendix). You'll want the one-pound can, which costs about $40. A quick-draw holster is a must.

Grizzlies

Grizzlies are shy animals and will usually run away from you. The grizzly is the king of the hill in its domain, so it's doubtful you can bluff one. I was once charged by three grizzlies on the open tundra of Canada, and I can vouch for the effectiveness of this procedure:

1. Talk in a moderate, non-threatening tone to the bear as you slowly back away. Do not make eye contact. Let the bear know that you made a mistake and are trying to skedaddle.

2. If the bear runs towards you, interpret this as curiosity, not a charge. Remember, bears don't see very well, and they can't smell you if you're downwind.

3. When the bear is within 50 feet, drop to the ground, face down, nose in the dirt, and clasp your hands tightly behind your head. Spread your legs wide so the bear can't turn you over easily. *Note:* Until recently, the recommended method

Camping   51

was to assume a tight fetal position, hands behind the head. I did this, and it worked for me. Discouraging bears is not an exact science.

New research by Stephen Herrero, author of *Bear Attacks*, Lyons & Burford, 1985, suggests that the face-down plan is best. Herrero found that the face is where most serious injury occurs. If the bear bites and claws you, try to remain quiet and passive. If the bear tries to flip you over, do a complete roll and maintain the face-down position. You will probably survive the attack.

Insects

Everyone knows the repellents are essential on most camping trips. But the color of your clothes is also important. Insects (especially mosquitoes) are attracted to dark colors, notably navy blue. Powder-blue, yellow, white, and most greens and reds are neutral. The light colors may, in fact, have a mild repellent effect.

If you're camping with children, choose a mild cream repellent rather than a more effective one which is high in DEET (N-N Diethyl-metatoluamide). Strong repellents may burn sensitive young skin. And, oh yes, keep repellents away from plastics: These products will instantly dissolve eyeglasses, polypropylene underwear, and the handles of Swiss Army knives.

Headnets are essential for early season trips in the northern states and Canada. You can make a headnet in a few minutes. Just sew up a wide rectangle of mosquito net, large enough to fit over your head and wide-brimmed hat. Make the net long enough to drape lazily on your shoulders.

It's difficult to see through milk-colored netting. If you can't find a dark-colored headnet, buy a light-colored one and darken the eye panel with black magic marker, dye, or spray paint.

Bug jackets. The Shoe-Bug jacket—available at most bait and tackle shops—offers state-of-the-art protection against all manner of biting insects. The jacket consists of a net fabric that you soak with pure DEET (which is allowed to dry). The repellent discourages insects and the cool mesh keeps them away from your body. It's the most effective anti-bug system available. There are also some non-DEET impregnated jackets, which are made from tightly woven cotton or no-see-um netting. These work as well as the Shoe-Bug models but are much hotter to wear.

Some Final Tips

1. Bugs will avoid your face if you saturate your bandanna with repellent and tie it loosely around your neck. Spray the underside of your hat brim, too.

2. Some of the most effective first-aid products for bug bites contain aloe, a plant-derived ingredient that has been around for thousands of years. Aloe soothes inflammation, inhibits swelling, and keeps skin moist. It also soothes burns and kills bacteria and fungi. To be effective, aloe should make up at least 80 percent of the product's formula.

3. If you have very sensitive skin and are concerned about using a DEET-based repellent, try a product that has citronella as an active ingredient. Citronella will repel "gentle insects" like mosquitoes, but it's not tough enough for black flies.

4. Liquid or cream repellents are much more potent (a better buy) than sprays.

5. Household ammonia and water will cut the sting of mosquito bites. For bee, wasp and hornet stings, apply a wet salt pack and allow it to dry. The salt will draw the pain away quickly.

Susie Bug Net

First, you apply DEET to all exposed skin. As more insects home in, you add a headnet, then a DEET-impregnated bug jacket. Ultimately, you rant and swear, then in disgust retire to your insect-proof tent. Meanwhile, friends nearby enjoy a bug-free after-dinner brandy and a glorious sunset inside their "Susie bug net"—personal-sized bug armor designed by my wife, Sue Harings.

Materials needed: A piece of mosquito netting 60 to 72 inches wide and 8 feet long, plus enough 1/8-inch diameter shock cord to span the hem. Don't use no-see-um net: It's not strong enough, and you can't see through it.

Procedure: Fold the netting lengthwise to produce a rectangular sheet that measures about 8 feet by 6 feet. Sew up the two long sides, hem the bottom and install the bungee cord in the hem. The finished net will weigh less than a pound and compress to football size.

HERE ARE SOME USES FOR YOUR SUSIE BUG NET:

1. Eat inside it; there's room for two.

2. Sleep out under the stars. The net covers you from head to toe. Remember to cinch the bungee cord tightly around the foot of your sleeping bag.

3. Use as a "portable outhouse" when bugs are bad.

4. Bathe in it! Amble to the beach as a ghostly apparition in your Susie bug net. Wear your life vest and you'll float confidently inside your bug armor.

5. Lay the net over breads, cheese, and lunch meats to keep flies away.

6. Rig a tripod inside and you have a tiny bug-proof tepee in which to wash dishes, cook, and make repairs.

Roll and stuff your Susie bug net under a pack flap, so it will be available at meals and river rest stops.

Note: **The Susie bug net is now being manufactured by Cooke Custom Sewing, Inc. (see Appendix).**

Ecological Concerns

Food leftovers should be bagged in plastic and packed out of the woods. When this is impractical, the best method of disposal is burning. Even soupy foodstuffs will burn if you add them a little at a time to a hot fire.

Burn all garbage *completely*, being sure to pick aluminum foil out of the flames. Burn out tin cans and flatten them with the back of your handaxe or rock, and pack them out.

Fish entrails should not be thrown into a waterway, where they will increase bacteria levels and reduce the supply of oxygen for fish. Instead, bury viscera 4 to 8 inches deep, as far as possible from the campsite. This relatively shallow depth is best for decomposition and also minimizes the possibility of it being dug up by animals. If there's only an inch or two of soil cover available, weight remains with a heavy rock or log.

Human waste should be buried four to eight inches deep too, (an aluminum tube with one end flattened makes a good shovel). Toilet paper and sanitary napkins should be burned, because these items require a full year or more to degrade.

And please don't throw food (or anything else) in Forest Service box latrines or chemical toilets. Bears commonly upset latrines to get at food. The mess that results is indescribable.

Dishes should be washed 100 feet away from a water source. Greasy dishwater is best poured into a small hole in the ground and covered with a few inches of soil. It should go without saying that you should never bathe (with soap) in any waterway.

Water Purification

If you value your health, you'll get your drinking water only from approved sources, or you'll treat it or carry it with you.

I confess to laziness in this respect. I despise the taste of chemically treated water; I don't like to mess with filters, and at eight pounds per gallon, I'll seldom carry more than a canteen full of water. Usually, I obtain my drinking water from a lake or river, though I'm very careful where I get it. Here are the guidelines I religiously follow:

1. Go well away from any shoreline to get drinking water. If you're camping at a spot that is frequented by man or animals, go upstream of the source to get your water. On lakes, a minimum of 100 feet from shore is recommended—and the farther out you go the better.

2. Decay organisms (bacteria, protozoans, and fungi) generally prefer the shallows, so the deeper your water source, the better.

3. Avoid any water with a greenish tinge. It contains algae and is usually loaded with microorganisms.

4. Don't take water from backwaters and stagnant areas. These are breeding places for microorganisms.

5. Don't drink any water that has been contaminated by wastes from a paper mill. Secure your water from incoming streams instead.

6. Don't take water near beaver dams or lodges. Beaver are the favored host of *Giardia lamblia*—a small protozoan that will make you plenty sick. The disease (called Giardiasis) is characterized by severe diarrhea, cramps, nausea, gas, and vomiting. Incubation time is generally one or two weeks, though some people have gone as long as two months without developing symptoms. If untreated, Giardiasis may go on for years. The disease is not at all easy to diagnose.

Field Methods of Water Treatment

Boiling. Most organisms are killed instantly when water reaches a rolling boil. A one-minute boil is usually adequate, except in problem areas or at high altitudes.

Portable filters. The vacuum-operated, portable filters sold at camping shops will produce quality water. Not all filters will remove *Giardia*.

Chemicals. Chemicals that release iodine or chlorine are available in tablet form from most pharmacies and camping shops. Generally, iodine is more effective than chlorine, especially on *Giardia*. However, neither compound works very well in cold or cloudy water.

Despite new chemicals and scientific filters, boiling remains the most reliable method for treating drinking water.

Ropemanship

Given enough rope—and time—anyone can rig a snug camp. Add a knife, and anyone can cut one down. Between these extremes are a small number of elite outdoorspeople who can match the right knot to the job at hand—and untie it instantly the morning after an all-night rain. Stroll through a wooded campground at season's end and count the number of tightly knotted cords you see hanging hopelessly from the vegetation and you'll understand the importance of ropemanship.

Outdoor handbooks define dozens of knots, most of which are quite useless in the woods. In reality, all you need to know are two knots and two hitches. Learn these well and you'll be at home in any situation, even those which require some rescue work.

Old-timers will note the conspicuous absence of the square knot and tautline hitch. Except for limited first-aid applications, the square knot is worthless; and the infamous tautline hitch—so useful in the days of cotton tents and manila rope—has now been replaced by the much more powerful and versatile power cinch.

The Double Half-Hitch *(Two Half-Hitches)*

The double half-hitch (Figure 7-1) is useful for tying a rope to a tree, as for a clothesline or to rig a tarp. The knot is very secure and tends to tighten itself when a load is applied. If you want to get this knot out quickly, finish it with a quick-release loop as shown in Figure 7-6.

The Sheet Bend

Use the sheet bend for tying two ropes together. The knot works well even when rope sizes are dissimilar. The sheet bend is about the only knot that can be used to join the ends of slippery polypropylene rope.

Figure 7-1
....

Double half-hitch.

Figure 7-2
....

Sheet bend.

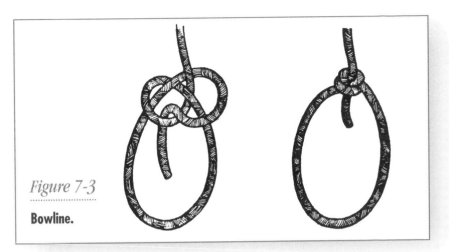

Figure 7-3

Bowline.

A friend once won five dollars when he fixed a broken water-ski towrope with this knot. When the towline snapped, the owner of the ski boat bet my friend he couldn't tie the two ends of the slick polypropylene rope together tightly enough to hold. No problem. My friend won the bet and skied the remainder of the day on the repaired line.

It's important that the free ends of the sheet bend be on the same side, as shown in Figure 7-2. The knot will work if the ends are opposite, but it will be less secure.

The Bowline

Here's an absolutely secure knot that won't slip regardless of the load applied. The bowline is the most important knot for mountain climbing. Use it whenever you want to put a nonslip loop on the end of a line or around your waist.

Beginners are often told to make the bowline by forming a loop, or "rabbit hole." The rabbit (free end of the rope) comes up through the hole, around the tree (opposite or long end of the rope shown in Figure 7-3) and back down the hole. The knot will slip a few inches before it tightens, so allow an extra-long free end.

Power Cinch

This ingenious hitch (Figure 7-4) works like a winch with a 2:1 mechanical advantage. Use it to secure the lines of a tent to a stake or tree (Figure 7-5) or to rig a drum-tight clothesline in camp. The power cinch is the hitch of choice whenever you need a secure tie-down. Carrying canoes on car tops, lashing furniture into the bed of pickup

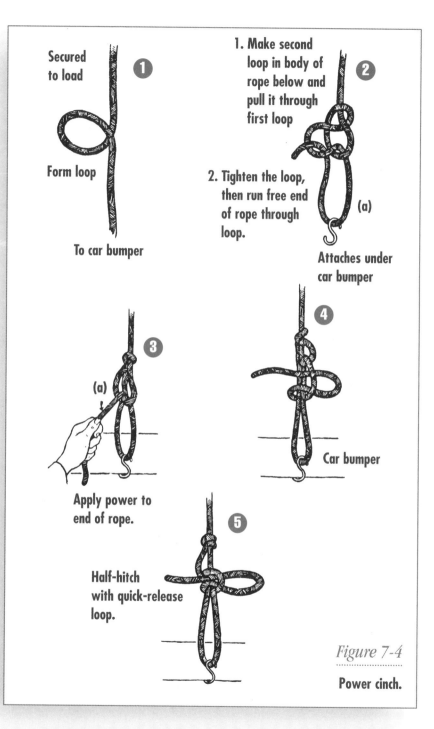

Secured to load

1

1. Make second loop in body of rope below and pull it through first loop

2

Form loop

2. Tighten the loop, then run free end of rope through loop.

To car bumper

(a)

Attaches under car bumper

3

(a)

4

Car bumper

Apply power to end of rope.

5

Half-hitch with quick-release loop.

Figure 7-4

Power cinch.

Figure 7-5

Secure your tent to a tree stake with a power cinch.

trucks, and tying tents and sleeping bags to aluminum pack frames are all useful applications of this versatile hitch.

Begin the power cinch by forming the loop shown in Figure 7-4, step 1. Pull the loop through as in step 2. It's important that the loop be formed exactly as shown. The loop will look okay if you make it backwards, but it won't work.

If the loop is formed as in step 2, a simple tug on the rope will eliminate it. This is preferable to the common practice of tying a knot in the loop, which, after being exposed to a load, is almost impossible to get out.

If you're tying a load in place on top of a car, tie one end of the rope to the load and snap the steel hook on the other end of the rope to the car's bumper—or, if you're using a car-top carrier, run the rope from bar to bar, using two half-hitches on one side and a power cinch on the other. Run the free end of the rope (a) through the loop in the power cinch (step 2), and apply power to the free end. You've created a pulley with a 2:1 mechanical advantage.

Complete the hitch by securing a double half-hitch around the body of the rope, or use a quick-release loop as illustrated.

The Quick-Release Loop

There's nothing more frustrating than untying a bunch of tight knots when you're breaking camp in the morning. If you end your knots with a quick-release loop like that illustrated in Figure 7-4, step 5, you'll be able to untie your lines with a single pull.

Form the quick-release feature by running the free end of the rope back through the completed knot—the same as making a "bow" when tying your shoes.

Use a simple overhand knot with a quick-release loop to seal the stuff sacks that contain your sleeping bag and personal gear (Figure 7-6). The plastic cord-locks sold for this purpose are for people who don't know how to tie effective quick-release knots.

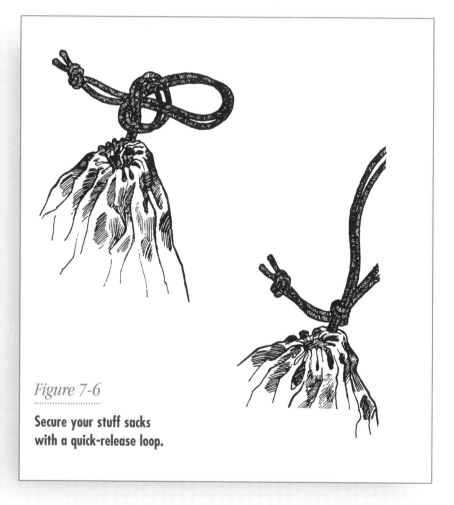

Figure 7-6

Secure your stuff sacks
with a quick-release loop.

Dangers

Everyone has heard grim tales about campers who have been lost in the woods, struck by lightning, crushed by a fallen tree, or drowned while swimming.

People who don't camp out react with horror to these stories and solemnly agree that the wild outdoors must be very dangerous. Experienced campers know better. In fact, most experienced outdoorspeople travel the bush for years without ever having an accident. There are occasional challenges, to be sure, but death-defying encounters are rare. Competent campers respect nature and have a proven battle plan to escape its dangers. They also have the skills to execute their plan.

Herein lies the secret of safe outdoor travel: Have the skills to carry out your battle plan!

Here are some common camping concerns.

Sprained Ankle

For years I got by with adhesive tape and an Ace bandage. Then my doctor gave me a lightweight air splint, which works much better. I've found that a person can walk confidently within minutes after spraining an ankle if he or she wears an air cast. Bring an air cast if you're going in harm's way.

Object in the Eye

Some years ago a woman in my canoeing class got sand beneath her contact lenses when her canoe capsized. The pain was unbearable. I gently lifted each eyelid and flushed out the particles with generous quantities of Eye Stream, a sterile irrigation solution. Then, I applied a ribbon of Polysporin ophthalmic ointment (Yellow oxide of mercury, ophthalmic 2 percent is the non-prescription alternative) inside each lower lid and immobilized the eyes with oval eye patches and microfoam tape. Finally, I administered Tylenol.

The woman said the pain ceased shortly after I applied the ointment. The next day she called to report that her doctor was so pleased with the treatment that he simply applied more ointment and replaced the bandages. Naturally, I was thrilled I had done things right.

Of all the medications in my kit, Polysporin ophthalmic ointment and large, oval eye patches have been most useful. I've used these several times to treat eye infections and scratched corneas.

Tip. **Eye patches are also great for patching blisters.**

Hypothermia—Killer of the Unprepared

The morning begins with a golden sun; by noon scattered clouds of twisted gray appear low on the horizon. Within the hour and icy drizzle falls. Curious, you look skyward, hopeful the discomfort will soon pass. But it doesn't. The rain continues. You snug the hood of your well-worn rain parka in hopes of discouraging the chilling drizzle, which has already soaked your cotton T-shirt and blue jeans. Soon, you begin to shiver, slightly at first, then uncontrollably. Ultimately, your speech thickens and you lose orientation. It's hard now to tell up from down, right from left. One minute you're walking drone-like down the muddy trail, the next, you're on your knees groping.

Total collapse comes an hour later. Suddenly, your sense of feel and awareness is gone. Shivering ceases, muscles become rigid; the once tender, pink skin becomes puffy white. You have penetrated the danger zone. Without help, you'll drift further into oblivion, towards death—the final goal.

Fortunately, knowledgeable friends are nearby and in command. Within minutes a tent is pitched and foam pads and bedding are placed inside. Wet clothes are stripped from your inanimate body and you are rushed to the awaiting sleeping bag where you are sandwiched—skin to skin—between two friends. Additional sleeping bags and parkas are pulled from their stuff sacks and piled over you. Nearby, someone struggles with a trail stove—hot soup is on the way.

The condition persists for many minutes, but ultimately your frigid body is re-warmed and you are able to sit up and talk intelligently. Now that you can swallow, you are given gentle sips of hot broth and are cheered back to your former state.

You are very lucky. Without such well directed, quick assistance, you surely would have died!

In the old days, they called it "exposure sickness". Now the technical term is *hypothermia*. But the cause—and symptoms—are the same. Hypothermia is a lowering of the body's core temperature. It may result from being plunged into cold water (immersion hypothermia), or from slow chilling, as in the above example.

The onset of hypothermia occurs when body temperature drops below about 95 degrees Fahrenheit. As blood is rushed to the vital organs, chilling spreads throughout the body. This is accompanied by clumsiness, slurred speech, and loss of judgment. Coma and death may occur with a few hours if the body temperature is not raised.

Most hypothermics are unaware of what is happening to them and will maintain an "I'm okay" attitude to the bitter end. It's up to other members of the party to observe the signals and take appropriate action.

Treatment for hypothermia consists of removing wet clothes and sandwiching the victim between two people in a sleeping bag, a la the illustrative example. Radiant heat from a fire may be used to speed the warming process, and is probably the quickest way to warm a hypothermic under typical field conditions. Be careful, though: Intense heat may burn the sensitive skin of the victim.

Hypothermia is physically and emotionally draining. Victims should be allowed to rest for a full day following the experience.

Your best protection against hypothermia is prevention. Select reliable rain gear and choose clothing that insulates well when wet. Wool is the traditional fabric, although polypropylene and pile work as well. Wet cotton literally wicks heat from the skin, so this fabric should never be worn in tricky weather. As mentioned, blue jeans are the worst thing you can wear in the backcountry.

Finally, keep the calories flowing while you hike. Constant nibbling on candy/nuts/granola, etc. will keep the temperature of your "furnace" high. If you get wet, stop immediately and change clothes. Many have died from hypothermia while clinging to the belief that they were saving their dry clothes for camp.

Lightning

The risk of being struck by lighting may be sharply reduced if you religiously follow these guidelines:

1. Lightning usually strikes the highest object in its path, so if you pitch your tent in an open field, be certain there are trees or rock formations of significantly greater height nearby.

2. A cone of protection extends from the tallest trees or landmass (as the case may be) about 45 degrees outward. Stay within this cone of protection, but far enough from its source so that lightning can't jump from the object to you.

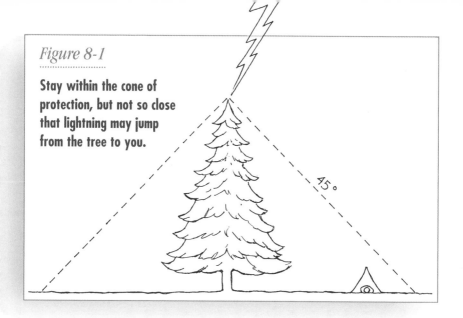

Figure 8-1

Stay within the cone of protection, but not so close that lightning may jump from the tree to you.

45°

Lightning may jump a dozen feet or more from the base of a tree, so don't crowd tall trees too closely. See Figure 8-1.

3. Lightning may travel along the roots of trees, which may extend dozens of feet outward. If roots are close to the surface of the ground, as in rocky areas where there is little soil cover, sufficient energy may be transmitted along subsurface roots to pose a danger to anyone standing on the ground above them. Keep this in mind when you pitch your tent!

4. If you're caught outside the cone of protection and suddenly feel electrical energy building (dry hair will stand on end), immediately get as low as possible to reduce the human lightning-rod effect.

5. If you're in a tent and lightning strikes all around, sit up immediately and draw your legs to your chest so that only your buttocks and feet touch the ground. A foam sleeping pad (preferably doubled) placed beneath you may provide enough insulation to keep you from being grounded.

You must maintain the recommended "sitting" position during an electrical storm. In the unlikely event you are struck by lightning while in this position, only your feet and buttocks are apt to burn. But if you're lying flat, the electricity may stop your heart!

Lightning usually kills people by stopping their heart. It may also paralyze the respiratory system. If your friend has been struck by lightning—and is alive—the burns are probably minor and you can attend to them later. The important thing is to *begin CPR immediately* and get the heart going again.

Electrocution may cause disorientation, coma, seizures, and spinal cord injuries. It may also rupture the eardrums. All you can do till help arrives is to keep your friend immobilized and warm and convince him that he'll be okay.

Widow Makers

Always check your campsite for tall leaning trees, especially dead or damaged ones, which may come crashing down on you in a windstorm. Old-time woodsmen call these leaning trees "widow makers." Can you guess why?

Some tree species are weaker than others. Watch out for soft maples (silver maple and box elder), which can split violently, and stands of young trees that are not protected from wind by bigger trees. Also, be wary of big old trees whose roots run very close to the surface of the ground.

Swimming

Swimming and camping trips naturally go together. But, please wear shoes of some sort when you take to water. The toughest feet are no match for rusty tin cans and broken bottles.

Getting Lost

Most beginning campers secretly admit a deep fear of getting lost in the woods and not being found. In truth, if you carry a knife and matches on all your outings, and can make a one-match fire (see page 24), you have little to fear. If you do get lost, stay put and build a huge smoky bonfire. Searchers will find you in a matter of hours or days.

It would be unfair to leave the subject of navigation without mentioning the wonderful new GPS (global positioning system) units (Figure 8-2) that are flooding the market. These battery-powered units receive signals from twenty-four orbiting satellites. With a civilian model GPS, you can locate your position (within 100 meters) anywhere on earth in a matter of minutes—if you can read a map, that is!

Outdoors people are buying GPS units like mad, though precious few know how to use them. To use a GPS effectively, you must first know how to read a map and compass. And, your maps must have a coordinate system that the GPS unit can understand.

If you're deadly serious about learning the GPS system, first learn how to use a map and compass. Then, read Michael Ferguson's excellent book, *GPS, Land Navigation* (Glassford Publishing, 1997).

Figure 8-2

A GPS unit.

Appendix

Bushwacker Backpack and
Supply Company
120 Industrial Court
Kalispell, MT 59901
(406) 257-4740

Cabela's Inc.
(800) 237-4444
Stores in Nebraska, Minnesota,
and Wisconsin

Cook Custom Sewing, Inc.
7290 Stagecoach Trail
Lino Lakes, MN 55014-1988
(612) 784-8777
fax: (612) 784-4158

Duluth Pack Store
365 Canal Park Drive
Duluth, MN 55802
(800) 849-4489
www.duluthpacks.com

Fast Bucksaw, Inc.
110 East Fifth Street
Hastings, MN 55033
(612) 437-2566

Idaho Knife Works
P.O. Box 144
Spirit Lake, ID 83869
(509) 994-9394

Sturdiwheat
321 Main Street
Red Wing, MN 55066
(800) 201-9650

Trailblazer
2736 Robie Street
Halifax, Nova Scotia B3K 4P2
(800) 565-6564

Z.Z. Corporation
10806 Kaylor Street
Los Alamitos, CA 90720
(800) 594-9046

Index

B A S I C   E S S E N T I A L

About The Author

Cliff Jacobson is one of North America's most respected outdoors writers and wilderness guides. He is a professional canoe outfitter and guide for the Science Museum of Minnesota and a wilderness canoeing consultant for Eckerd Family Youth Alternatives, Inc. When he's not canoeing, Cliff also teaches eighth grade environmental science as well as Wilderness Experience, a program he developed for students at risk. He is strongly committed to the ethics of "leave no trace" camping.

Cliff has authored sixteen outdoors books and numerous educational publications, including *Canoeing Wild Rivers,* considered by many to be one of the most authoritative resources of its kind. Three of his titles were among the top ten best-selling outdoors books in 1996. He has also written for the Minnesota Department of Natural Resources, and he developed the orienteering materials for Minnesota schools. His water-quality program, Water Water Everywhere, written for the Hach Co., is widely used in schools, and his Wilderness Meal program is an extremely popular environmental education activity.